4.00

W9-CKK-378

VEGETABLES
MONEY CAN'T BUY
BUT YOU CAN GROW

Vegetables money can't buy

but
you can grow

NANCY WILKES BUBEL

 DAVID R. GODINE
BOSTON

First published in 1977 by
DAVID R. GODINE, PUBLISHER
306 Dartmouth Street
Boston, Massachusetts

Copyright © 1977 by Nancy Wilkes Bubel

No part of this book may be used or reproduced in any manner
whatsoever without written permission except in the case of
brief quotations embodied in critical articles and reviews.

DESIGNED BY PHILIP GRUSHKIN

The editors would like to thank the following for their
help with the illustrations for this book:
The W. Atlee Burpee Company
The Golden Archives, New York
The Gray Herbarium Library, Harvard College
Joseph Harris Seed Company
The Schlesinger Library, Radcliffe College
R. H. Shumway, Seedsman

Printed in the United States of America

VEGETABLES MONEY CAN'T BUY has been smyth sewn
rather than glued. The book opens flat for easy reference, the
pages will not fall out, and the binding will endure years of
hard use by all sorts of gardeners.

Dedicated to my husband,

MICHAEL

CONTENTS

PART ONE

Vegetables money can't buy

PART TWO

but you can grow

A NOTE
TO THE
READER

This book is meant to be a guide to selecting and growing the uncommon vegetables of exceptional merit—vegetables that are the special province and delight of the home gardener. Most of the vegetables mentioned may be grown from coast to coast and border to border. There's nothing regional about them. Whether your cooking style centers around wholly natural foods, homestyle meat and potatoes, vegetarian or ethnic-experimental meals, or the classic gourmet dishes involving shallots, wine and special sauces, I hope you'll find here new vegetables worth growing for your table and new ways of using old favorites.

There is an old Japanese saying:

Whenever
you try a new food,
you add seventy-five days
to the length
of your
life.

What more could I wish for you, gardening friends!

ACKNOWLEDGMENTS

Once I read a gardening book that claimed to have in it no information from the library shelf—everything was worked out from personal experience. I know there are few days in the year when I do not have my hands in the soil, one way or another. But in the evenings, I read up on what I've been doing, looking for new and better (or sometimes older and surer) ways of working my garden. Books have been important to me; applying and experimenting with what I've learned has made our vegetable garden much more productive.

And so it follows that I am indebted, in tangled ways impossible to trace, to authors of the many gardening books I've consulted for advice on my own garden, to helpful editors and gardening friends, to readers of my articles who have asked questions and shared experiences and to those whose gardens I've glimpsed in passing. Thank you, good people. If you see your influence in these pages, know that I am grateful.

I am especially grateful to Richard M. Ketchum, editor of *Country Journal*, for his permission to reprint, as part of this book, material originally published in the April 1975 issue of *Country Journal*.

A good share of the credit for our own productive vegetable garden must go to my husband Mike and our children, Mary Grace and Gregory, who have cheerfully helped to haul and spread mulch and manure. Their enthusiasm for trying new things has made raising vegetables money can't buy a most satisfying endeavor.

NANCY BUBEL
Wellsville, Pennsylvania
May 1977

13

WHEN DID YOU LAST SEE SPAGHETTI SQUASH FOR SALE IN YOUR LOCAL MARKET?

How about sugar peas, burpless cucumbers, or vegetable soybeans, small, new, crunchy kohlrabi, mild savoy cabbage, low-acid tomatoes or, for that matter, plum tomatoes? I won't even ask whether you can buy leaf lettuce, salsify, leeks or Oriental radishes. Unless your town hosts a farmers' market or a wharfside vendors' street, you aren't likely to find any of these delicacies for sale.

The trouble is that quality doesn't keep. Vegetables sold in store bins are selected by the store because they will hold up in storage. Perhaps they are as good as they might ever have been. But a whole margin of flavor (to say nothing of food value) is missing. It was never there in the first place.

We are, you see, at the mercy of a hugely efficient system of food distribution. Truck farms no longer cluster around our cities and towns, bringing fresh, locally-grown produce to food markets. No, the vegetables displayed on your supermarket's produce counter—though they may be sprinkled periodically to look dewy fresh—were *not* picked yesterday on the edge of town. They were, more likely, picked last week halfway across the country. The average chicken, I understand, travels 3,000 miles from producer to consumer. How astonishing to think of vegetables so well-travelled!

The whole system of food distribution is a marvel of organization and standardization. The eggplant and broccoli you buy this week will be of about the same quality as that you bought last week. No odd vegetables, no blemishes, no insect damage—true. But—equally true—no succulence, mediocre flavor, questionable vitamin content, invisible but significant pesticide and fungicide residue.

We are amazed that we can buy, year-round, produce that we could once get only "in season." We have forgotten that special quality only "in season" food has: a chain-store cabbage tastes pretty much the same, winter and summer.

You can't blame the chain store entirely. In response to grower demand, seed firms have developed varieties of vegetables that are especially tough and fibrous, so that they will withstand mechanical picking. It is the natural habit of vegetables, when they are picked, to release organic compounds called volatile esters; when the esters have gone, so has the flavor. As a matter of practical necessity, vegetables that must be shipped long distances in large amounts are chosen for their longevity in transit rather than for their intrinsic flavor and nutrition. Even vegetables that have wilted once may be cosmetically revived, but they have suffered irreparable losses of vitamins.

All this efficiency costs something. In addition to losses of flavor, variety, nutrition and personal choice, there are also the tremendous fuel costs involved in all that trucking around and in the packaging and cooling so necessary to this system of distribution. So you really do end up paying more for less.

But things are not hopeless! Unlike so many of the problems currently frustrating us, this one can be solved, on the personal level at least, by people—individual people—taking matters once more into their own hands and growing, in their own yards, what they like. It's as simple and as revolutionary as that. Perhaps only when you take a hand in providing your own food do you have a real choice, after all.

As everyone knows, raising your own vegetables saves money. An average backyard patch can easily produce vegetables worth $200 to $300 over growing costs. It is less commonly known, though, that you can grow food which in most places can't be bought at any price. Most of us equate thrift with "making do," but gardeners have the best of both worlds: while raising produce that costs little more than their labor, they can feast on the delicate flavors, the perfect textures, the extra food values of vegetables not to be obtained elsewhere.

When you grow your own, a whole new world of real food becomes available to you. Perhaps you don't care for wax on your cucumbers, nitrates in your spinach, or pesticides on your lettuce. Neither do I. When you've known your vegetables from the ground up, you can be sure that they are wholesome—all the way through. What is perfection, after all? Uniformity, dependability, freedom from blemish?

16

. . . or wholesomeness, superb flavor, fine texture, good food value? Who cares how well your vegetable keeps or ships? You'll eat it the day it's picked!

If—like us—you want to store your own vegetables for a year-round supply, you'll find in the following pages home garden vegetables that hold their quality indefinitely when kept under the right conditions. Then, despite the early winter dark, the dinner table is bright with baked squash from the cellar, beets and kale from the garden, and pickled beans and peppers from the canning shelf. Add parsley from the cold frame or windowsill and sauerkraut from the crock on the cold back porch . . . and you'll hardly have room for the pork chops sputtering on the stove!

In the seventeen years we've been raising vegetables, we've had a consistent harvest of produce we could never have found otherwise —sweet, snappy sugar peas; kohlrabi picked young, as it should be; delicate, crisp leaf lettuce; tender, green vegetable soybeans with all the goodness of limas and no starch. The only vegetables we ever buy are an occasional midwinter stalk of celery, a sack of potatoes or onions if we run out before spring, and an early spring bunch of asparagus (our asparagus bed is still too young to produce heavily).

You don't need a big spread in order to grow fresh vegetables for your family. A well-planned backyard garden, rented community plot or borrowed corner on a relative's land can keep you in good eating all season long. We've known apartment dwellers who raised salad greens on balconies and town house owners who had fresh tomatoes at their front doorstep. Whatever your reasons for putting in a garden —taste, nutrition, economy, recreation—you'll likely discover that a garden with a few special vegetables can be not only a sensible way to economize but a real gourmet pleasure.

There's another thing about vegetables too. When green beans *and* corn *and* tomatoes are ripe, you're likely to eat all three at the same meal. Fresh salads become a daily treat on the gardener's table. You may well find that you don't need rich desserts and snack foods— not when the vegetables are so good and so plentiful. And the newly recognized value of food fiber provides one more good reason for serving plenty of fresh, fiber-rich, homegrown vegetables. You just might find, after a season of growing and eating fresh garden vegetables, that you're in better shape than ever!

One more note, then on to the vegetables. In place of the usual weather maps or charts and tables for frost dates and growing conditions (which you can find for yourself in any library), I've tried to think in terms of "look around you" rather than "look it up." Plants set out strictly by the calendar may be laid low by severe winds or a late snowstorm. I'd suggest instead learning to see and sense what other plants and creatures are up to. Take your cues from trees, birds, spring peepers, bees. I'm trying to learn this technique too and find they often know, far better than we, when the time is right.

Here on our mountainside farm, for instance, I've noticed temperatures are consistently lower than in nearby cities. Even within the farm there are patches that warm more quickly than others. When we lived and gardened in the city, sheltered by close buildings and big old trees, we enjoyed milder temperatures than suburban relatives just a few miles away.

Ask the old-timers among your neighbors about these things. They most likely know how the seasons run. One of our favorite elderly gardeners always waits until the barn swallows return to plant out his tomatoes. I've been watching . . . it looks as though he knows what he's talking about. Observe your own garden and keep notes on it from year to year. Then, rather than a rigid instant formula, you'll have a gradually emerging pattern of interrelationships to refer to: something generated by your surroundings, not imposed upon them.

Look, feel, listen. Take it all in. Happy planting and happy gardening!

Vegetables
money
can't
buy

BEANS

Phaseolus vulgaris—bush beans

Almost everyone likes green beans. The basic bean is, of course, generally available in stores. But how about the full-flavored broad bean? Do Blue Lake beans exist outside of cans? Do you know what's good about purple beans? Have you tried Wade and Contender, considered by some to be the best-flavored beans of all? These are beans that you'll find only in the garden patch, and they include some of the best.

We begin our planting season with the purple beans, available from many seed companies as Royalty beans. Royalty's ancestral bean, Blue Coco, is a French variety of pole bean that dates back 200 years. Also purple podded, it is worth growing for its good flavor if you want to send for imported seeds. (See Sources, page 129.) The American strain of Royalty was selected and developed by Professor E. M. Meader of the University of New Hampshire from seed handed down through the years in a family of New England gardeners.

Royalty seeds may be planted several weeks earlier than those of other beans, since they will germinate and grow in the cool, damp weather which would rot off other bean seed. They are still frost-tender though, so don't plant the seed more than three weeks before the date of your last expected spring frost. Most years we are eating our own fresh "purple green beans" by the end of June, thanks to that early start. The blossoms of the purple bean are a beautiful shade of lavender and the beans themselves a surprising rich purple, easy to find when picking. They turn the familiar green when cooked. The texture and flavor are excellent, and hold up for freezing as well as that of any other bean.

Another green bean that seems to be a gardener's exclusive is the

21

Italian bean, called Romano in most catalogues, but known also as Bachicha. Available in both pole and bush forms, this bean bears flat, wide pods about five inches long and three-quarters of an inch wide. Though the pole beans get off to a slower start, they produce over a longer period of time. The distinctive rich flavor and melting texture are pretty much the same in both forms.

While these beans may be purchased frozen in small packages, they have never been offered in fresh form anywhere I've shopped. I'm willing to wager that one taste of fresh beans right from your garden will spoil you for the rest of the season. And the cost of a meal's worth of frozen beans will pay for seed that will provide a continuous supply of fresh ones.

22

We plant inoculated bush bean seed two inches apart and thin the plants to stand about five inches apart. (Inoculation is a simple procedure. Just shake a few pinches of garden pea and bean inoculant, available at hardware stores and through seed catalogues, over the moistened seed and shake to distribute it evenly. The nitrogen-fixing bacteria in the powder will transform nitrogen from the air into a form the plant can readily absorb, thereby nourishing the plant and enriching the soil for the crop that will follow.) For pole beans, we set a row of rough, eight-foot poles about three feet apart and plant about eight seeds around each pole, thinning the group later to retain the best four to five plants. Early planted bush beans often bear a good crop before the bean beetle attacks. Midseason crops usually suffer rather heavy bean beetle damage but the last planting—in early summer for an early fall crop—seems to fare best of all. Rotenone does control the bean beetle to some extent, but it is difficult to get complete coverage on the undersides of the leaves where the soft-bodied larvae lurk. Hand-picking of the varmints, most easily done while harvesting the beans, is well worth the few extra minutes it takes.

When the beans start to come on, we eat them every day without tiring of them. We freeze and pickle a good many quarts of beans for the winter, but we try not to let that process interfere with our daily enjoyment of the fresh beans in their prime. In our opinion, the easy commercial availability of out-of-season (and often flavorless) foods has led to an unrealistic expectation of endless menu variety. Perhaps it is only mediocrity that needs to be varied. For our part, we enjoy concentrating on beans while the beans are good, feasting for a week on corn at the peak of sweetness, dining daily on tomatoes too juicy and thin-skinned to ship, eating the day's pick of sugar peas in celebration of June . . . they're never the same again.

BEETS

Beta vulgaris

Beets are such agreeable vegetables. They may be planted early and late, they take little room, and they are seldom bothered by diseases or insect pests. Both the top and the root are good to eat; beet greens are, in fact, lower in calories and higher in vitamins than the roots we customarily consider to be the main crop.

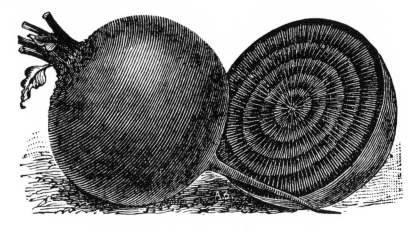

"But," you say, "I can buy beets at the store." And so you can—bunching beets grown for uniformity of size and visual appeal. No one would try to sell commercially the large, unkempt, rough-looking Long Season beet. Its tenderness and fine grain are a secret known only to gardeners. And who would know by its appearance that the Golden beet is sweet, full of flavor, and does not bleed as red beets do? Any market that put the long, slim Cylindra beet on the produce rack would have a lot of explaining to do. That's not what beets are supposed to look like! Cylindra, though, is a fine-textured beet that holds its quality well and slices perfectly for pickling.

Besides, when you *buy* beets, the greens have usually been lopped off. (By the time they reached the market they were in no shape to eat, anyway!) When you grow your own, you have only yourself to blame if you miss out on those nutritious greens!

In most parts of the country you can plant beets a month before the last frost. In far northern areas where the last frost of the season may still be a hard, killing one, it might be wise to delay seeding until about two weeks before the last expected frost date.

The beet seeds we plant are really corky balls containing three to seven small seeds. That's why they always need thinning, no matter how carefully you measure the three-inch spacing when you plant them. After planting, firm the ground well over the row to assure close contact of the rough seed with the moist soil. This seems to be especially important for beets. For beets of the best quality, plant small amounts of seed frequently. The Long Season beet should be planted early. Beets are at their best when grown rapidly, since in hot, dry summers they tend toward woodiness, but this particular beet keeps very well and tastes good even when big and ungainly looking.

24

Be sure to make a late summer planting too, in July or August, for tender new fall beets.

Unlike most other root vegetables, beets don't mind being transplanted. It slows them up, of course, but then your harvest continues over a longer period of time. As with all transplanting, a cloudy, damp day is the best time for the job. Some gardeners dip the roots in a slurry of thick, muddy water to protect them. Some also snip off the thready tip of the beet's taproot before resetting the seedling. This sounds drastic, but how many of us get those taproots in straight when transplanting 100 of them? Trimming the root tip not only helps to encourage the new beet root to grow straight; it also stimulates the formation of new feeder roots. Transplanting beets is hard on the knees but usually worth it, since you can often plant an additional row of beets from the thinnings you've removed.

If you'd rather not transplant, though, those tender young thinnings are delicious steamed for supper or added to the soup pot.

Beets are unusually sensitive to toxic substances in the soil. We discovered this the year we planted a row of beets at the end of the garden near an English walnut tree. Walnut roots exude juglone, a toxic substance that inhibits plant growth. *Inhibited* . . . ours didn't even germinate!

Otherwise, beets are troubled very little by insects or disease. A lack of boron in the soil will cause bitter black spots in the roots. The officially recommended remedy for this is to dissolve one-half teaspoon of borax in twelve gallons of water and sprinkle it on the row. But it seems to us that if such a small amount of the substance in such a large amount of water is effective, it would be all too easy to apply too much. A more gradual, long-lasting approach is to dig in, or compost and then apply, leaves of plants like cantaloupe, vetch and sweet clover, known to accumulate boron in the soil. Granite dust is also a good source for the necessary traces of boron.

CABBAGE

Brassica oleracea capitata—heading
B. chinensis—leafy Oriental
B. pekinensis—heading Oriental

Only the gardener may choose among cabbages. Certain varieties of cabbage, grown for their exceptionally mild, pleasing flavor, just aren't available at the store. Ask any gardening gourmets what cabbages they grow for good flavor. Chances are that Early Jersey Wakefield will be among their favorites. Or perhaps they will mention Savoy, the kind with the crinkled leaves, long grown as a milder alternative to the smooth-headed cabbage. The variety Savoy King is excellent.

For those who relish a stout, pungent, pickled cabbage, there are several red varieties—beautiful both in the row and on the plate. Ruby Ball is early, compact and solid, with a short core. Mammoth Red Rock is everything its name implies and stores well. Both do well in a condiment that will brighten your winter days. Chop two small heads (or one large one) of red cabbage. Add one cup of chopped onions, one tablespoon of salt and your favorite sweet-and-sour syrup. (Some cooks use three cups of vinegar and one and a half cups of sugar to make the syrup. We prefer to substitute one cup of honey for the sugar.) Simmer the combined ingredients for ten minutes and pack, boiling hot, into sterilized canning jars. Seal while hot. A delicious pickle!

Devotees of Chinese cuisine will want to grow one of the leafy

Oriental cabbages like Bok Choy, which tastes just as good with meat and potatoes as it does with rice and almond chicken. Like the onion, Chinese cabbage is sensitive to day length. Varieties Wong Bok, Michili and Chihili require short days for proper development; they should be planted in early summer for fall harvest. Some newer Japanese hybrids like Takii's Spring may be sown in spring with good results, but Chinese cabbage should be treated as a summer-planted fall crop.

Though you can make sauerkraut of any cabbage, even red, varieties with loosely-wrapped leaves are more difficult to grate. Real kraut lovers should plant one of the longer-growing, extra-large, solid varieties, good for shredding. Penn State Ballhead, Stonehead, Danish Ballhead, Flat Dutch and Merion Market are good kraut cabbages.

Cabbage is easy to grow. Since our soil tends to be acidic, we plant

27

our cabbage in a part of the garden on which we have recently spread limestone. We also give our cabbage plenty of nitrogen to promote leaf development. Those solid heads, you remember, are really tight clusters of leaves. Manure tea and diluted fish emulsion fertilizer are both excellent cabbage boosters.

You can plant cabbage seed in the garden as soon as the soil can be worked. Or you can get a jump on the season by starting plants indoors and setting them out when your garden patch is workable, even though nights are still frosty. Set the plants two feet apart in rows two feet apart, except for Jersey Wakefield and its yellows-resistant form, Jersey Queen. (Some areas of the country are troubled by yellows, a fungus disease that causes stunting and yellowing of the plant.) These small early conical heads may be spaced more closely.

Chinese cabbage grows an erect cylindrical head much like cos lettuce. It too may be planted at about eighteen-inch intervals. Most varieties of Chinese cabbage are susceptible to transplanting shock, which can cause them to bolt to seed, so follow every precaution if you do transplant them. Plants grown for fall use will most likely be seeded in the row and then thinned.

If space is limited, cabbage for your fall crop may be set in the same row that grew your early peas, if you use one of the earlier maturing varieties and set out started plants. This practice makes good use of the nitrogen left in the soil by the peas.

Cabbage, being shallow rooted, needs a steady supply of moisture, especially when heading. It grows best in cool weather. Spring planted cabbage must be picked rather promptly when the heads mature, but the fall crop lasts longer in the sun.

Like most gardeners, we've had the disheartening experience of seeing beautiful round cabbage heads split open after a heavy rain. Splitting can often be prevented, though, by gently pulling on the plant to break some of the feeder roots and thus reduce the amount of moisture the cabbage can absorb.

In early summer, the white cabbage butterfly hovers over the row of just-heading cabbages. We could enjoy the delicate summery picture they make if we didn't know that they're laying eggs which will hatch into hungry green larvae—cabbage worms. Our best defense against cabbage worms is a good early start on our cabbage plants so that they are forming solid heads when the worms hatch. Then the larvae are less likely to penetrate the firm inner core, and damage is confined to the outer leafy layers of the head. We always have plenty of cabbages in spite of the worms, but if they aren't leaving anything for you, try one of the following: dust the heads with rye flour or shake salt into the cabbages while they're dewy; put several spoonfuls of sour milk into each cabbage; or apply *Bacillus thuringiensis*, a highly selective bacterial control toxic to larvae of many moths and butterflies.

CARROTS

Daucus carota sativa

You can grow carrots like none you could ever buy. Shipped-in carrots must be smooth, uniformly sized and durable in storage. That's all that's really expected of them. Flavor? Tenderness? Sweetness? If you want all *that*, you must grow your own.

Homegrown carrots are often far from uniform, but that can be an advantage too. The little fingerlings may be cooked whole in stew; the

picture-perfect roots take on a fine brown glaze when roasted with meat; and the thick, gnarled ones are handy for making carrot salad: add one cup of raisins, one-half teaspoon salt, one tablespoon lemon juice, one cup mayonnaise (all the better if homemade!) and one can of drained, unsweetened, crushed pineapple to each four cups of grated carrot.

Carrots have been bred to grow in dependably distinctive shapes too. There's Short and Sweet, a new variety three to four inches long and two inches wide at the top that produces well in either heavy or shallow soil. Gold Nugget, about the size and shape of a golf ball, makes a splendid addition to the relish tray. Diminutive "baby finger" carrots, a bit larger than your little finger, are just the right size for pickling or canning whole.

Full-sized carrots run from the long, pointed Imperator to the short, stumpy Oxheart, a heavy yielder that keeps well. Danvers Half-Long, which reaches a length of about seven inches, rates high on flavor, yield and keeping quality, and will adapt to different soils. Scarlet Nantes, another seven-inch variety, grows a brittle carrot, cylindrical and blunt. Red-Cored Chantenay, about six inches long, has a large core and does well on heavy soil. And then there is Tendersweet, an extra sweet, small-cored carrot that's about as good as you can get—a real home gardener's special.

Carrots are easy to grow, take little space and have few insect pests. You can plant them early in the spring, but don't plant them first. Get your peas and onions in the ground; then plant carrot seed a week or two after the soil gets dry enough to dig.

Carrots like cool weather and a deeply dug plot with loose soil. If your soil is heavy or shallow, choose one of the many good shorter carrots like Oxheart, Danvers Half-Long or Red-Cored Chantenay that do well in such ground.

Carrot seed is very fine and practically impossible to avoid over-planting unless you mix it with sand or dry coffee grounds or buy pelleted seed (which hasn't worked too well for me). An average packet of regular seed will plant thirty feet of row; an ounce should be enough for at least 200 feet of row. If your soil doesn't have too many perennial weeds, you might want to try growing carrots in a row from four to twelve inches wide. You must weed these wide rows repeatedly and thoroughly while the seedlings are small, but when the foliage begins to amount to something, it will help keep the soil cool and shade out weedy competition. Whatever the width of your row, cover the seeds with one-quarter inch of fine soil—never more than one-half inch. Single rows should be spaced twelve to sixteen inches apart.

Carrot seed germinates two to three weeks after planting. Just about the time you've given up on them, you'll notice a faint line of delicate, ferny seedlings. Many gardeners plant radish seeds with the carrots— every four to six inches or so—to mark the row and to break the soil crust so that the little seedlings can emerge more easily.

Even if you've spaced out your seed with sand or some other extender, your carrots will almost certainly need thinning. I always wait to thin until the tops have become sturdy enough to grasp easily. Aim for a two-inch space between the average-sized plants. Large, late storage carrots may need as much as four inches.

Although carrots do best in cool weather, they *can* be laid low by a sudden really severe frost. To ensure a steady supply of carrots in peak form, make repeated plantings every few weeks from early spring until July. When planting in summer, I always water the trench first, scatter the seed and then draw a half-inch layer of fine dry soil over the seeds. A final sprinkling of dried grass clippings along the row helps prevent crusting of the soil after rain.

The insect problem you're most likely to run into with carrots is damage to the root by the tunnelling larvae of the carrot rust fly. Crops planted after the first week in June often escape the attack of the first generation of larvae, and those harvested before September are usually not hit by the second generation. If the larvae seem to be taking more than their share of the carrots in your garden, starve out (or at least confuse!) future generations by moving your carrot and celery rows to another part of the garden the following season.

Unlike some other fine garden vegetables, carrots will remain in good condition for some weeks. You needn't worry about missing their moment of perfection. They will keep well for winter eating too, either in boxes of damp sawdust in a cold cellar or right in the ground, covered with a foot of mulch. Thick-cored carrots are the best keepers. Eat the more tender thin-cored kinds first. And see if you don't agree that homegrown carrots can be as flavorful as they are colorful.

CAULIFLOWER

Brassica oleracea botrytis

Did you ever see a purple cauliflower? Surprising, just like purple beans. It looks like a big purple nosegay. The purple cauliflower needs no blanching. When cooked, it turns light green. The flavor is over on the broccoli side of cauliflower—very good! Perhaps the purple color throws the insects off the track, for we've never had much trouble with insect predators when we've grown this vegetable.

Self-Blanche is another good cauliflower. Ordinarily, the developing head of white cauliflower is covered by tying the outer leaves over it to prevent formation of chlorophyll. When Self-Blanche is grown to mature in cool weather, the leaves grow over the head naturally, making all that tying unnecessary. The flavor is delicate and mild — good either raw in salads or with a dip, or steamed, buttered and served with colorful food (but not, for example, with rice or mashed potatoes and fish!).

Cauliflower grows best when kept cool and moist, but it is more sensitive to frost than cabbage is. Since it cannot be planted out as early as cabbage, most gardeners raise it as a fall crop, setting out started plants in late spring. Space the plants eighteen to twenty inches apart in rows two to three feet apart.

Cauliflower has a highly developed sense of personal insult. If it suffers a setback at transplanting time — or if growth is checked at any stage of development — it is likely to become stunted, producing nothing more than a button head. You can see, then, that it is important to take extra good care of the roots when setting out transplants.

Keep a good ball of earth around each root, water the plant immediately, and shade the seedling from hot sun for a few days after transplanting. If any seedlings have bare roots, dip them in a slurry of thick, muddy water to coat the delicate feeder roots. Keep the plant growing steadily by mulching and watering during dry periods. Give the plant good rich soil with plenty of manure and limestone dug in.

Cauliflower's insect enemies are the same ones that visit cabbage; follow the same methods of control.

Harvest cauliflower when the heads are solid and fully "flowered" but before the stalks branch and the curd-like growth turns ricey. See if you don't notice a vast difference in flavor between your just-picked cauliflower and one that has been on the road for a week.

CELERIAC

Apium graveolens rapaceum

Why is it that we insist on defining untried vegetables in terms of those already familiar to us, in an attempt to make them more acceptable? Celeriac tastes like . . . celeriac: it has the tang of celery with a slightly sweet earthiness that makes it seem cousin to the beet or turnip. Actually, it is a form of celery grown for its bulbous root rather than for the stalks.

Celeriac is an old vegetable, commonly considered a staple in Europe. A marsh plant by nature and heritage, it thrives on heavy, moist, well-drained soil but is less sensitive to heat and drought than celery. It is used in much the same way as the outer ribs of celery—in soups, stews and casseroles. Indeed, if celery doesn't do well in your garden and you miss its flavor in soups, celeriac is a good substitute. It may also be grated, raw, into salads, or made into something like potato salad, with the customary dressing, onion, seasonings and hard-boiled egg slices, but substituting cooked and sliced celeriac for the potato. Or you might try equal portions of cooked, cubed celeriac and potatoes, following your usual recipe for potato salad.

Celeriac seed may be sown indoors about eight weeks before weather becomes settled, and the seedlings planted out after apple petals fall. Set the plants about six inches apart in rows eighteen inches apart. Some gardeners remove the small lateral roots near the top of the crown in order to produce a finer-grained celeriac root. Seed may also be planted directly in a row for a fall crop. Either way, it will be around

33

for awhile: it needs 120 days to mature. Don't give up; the seed itself takes two to three weeks to germinate. Try to keep the soil moist during that time. Lightly toss a few grass clippings over it to prevent crusting.

Although celeriac occupies a garden row for most of the growing season, it will remain in good condition in a root cellar or earthed-up storage box, well into the winter. The future may well demand that we provide for ourselves, year-round, as simply as possible; celeriac's flavor and good keeping qualities should assure it a place in the next generation of gardens.

CHIVES

Allium schoenoprasum

Usually classified as an herb, chives are a staple for us, so I consider it as a vegetable. We grow our chives by the kitchen doorstep, so that

34

it's easy to dash out for a fresh snipping just as we put our dinner on the table. We snip chives onto just about everything except ice cream: steaming potato soup, just ladled into bowls; bread fresh from the oven, slathered first with butter or cream cheese; cole slaw, cottage cheese, baked potatoes . . .

As you know, chive is a member of the onion family. Its slender, quill-like leaves, miniatures of the broader, coarser onion tops, spring from tiny bulbs that form a clump in a well-established plant. The plant blooms in early summer with a delicate lavender flower.

Once when we were camping, I bought a little envelope of freeze-dried chives to sprinkle on our breakfast eggs. I never bought another. As far as we can tell, the flavor of chives doesn't come through well when it's frozen or dried; at least our own experiments with it have been pleasantly green but disappointingly tasteless.

The only good chives, we've concluded, are fresh chives. That's no problem, even for the window-box gardener, for the plant is a perennial that amiably accepts most any climate and soil, as long as it has good sun and a fairly steady supply of moisture. It survives cold northern winters and grows fast in the cool early days of spring. Good

rich garden soil, with plenty of organic matter dug in, will keep the plant growing steadily all season long. It is a good idea to divide clumps of chives when they have grown in the same spot for three years. Set them a little deeper and make four plants where you formerly had one.

Food markets do occasionally sell pots of chives—usually in early spring, just when you need them most. They're worth buying and setting out; that one plant, well cared for, can supply you for years.

One clump is not enough for most chive lovers, though. Happily, they are easy to raise from seed; a packet will supply you and most of your neighbors. Start them in flats indoors, even in the dead of winter. The slender whip-like seedlings, resembling blades of grass, should be transplanted at least once before you set them out in the garden. They make an attractive border around perennial plantings. If you have the space, they deserve a spot of their own where they're not likely to be lost in the yearly upheaval of digging the garden. Protect them from weedy competition for the first two months, until they begin to form small sturdy clumps that tempt you to snip them.

Chives may just sit still and hold their own if not watered in a dry summer, but fall rains and cooler weather will send them into another burst of growth. For a winter supply of chives, you can pot up young plants and grow them in the house, either on a sunny windowsill or under lights. It's best to do this rather early in the fall so that the plant can adjust to indoor conditions before furnaces and fireplaces are necessary. It may take a little doing, but it's entirely possible to have a year-round supply of fresh chives—a gourmet touch that only a gardener could afford.

COMFREY
Symphytum officinale

Tea, herb, healing plant . . . comfrey is all of these, but it is also, for us, an outstanding vegetable. Once you get a good start with comfrey, you'll always have it. It's not only perennial, it's practically ineradicable. It owes its persistence to an extremely deep and strong root. If you dig up a comfrey plant, you'll never find each root fragment, and a finger-sized piece of root left in the ground is all the plant needs to start another crown.

So don't plant comfrey in the main vegetable garden. But do plant *some*, because it is nourishing, trouble-free, mild-flavored and available fresh from early spring through late fall. It is so mild, in fact, that when cooked it tastes very bland. We find this a valuable trait, though, since it can be mixed with peppery mustard, turnip or wild greens to tone them down. In preparing comfrey for a dinner vegetable, I usually braise the chopped leaves in oil along with sliced onions. It takes a generous amount of oil and lots of stirring to fix this dish, but it is good. To serve comfrey in a vegetable soup, just cook the finely snipped leaves right in the stock.

Comfrey is a good addition to a green salad too, unless you happen to object to the hairiness of its leaf. Last summer, while trying to build up his defenses for the coming hay-fever season, my husband developed an inspired way of eating fresh comfrey: fold the leaf in half along the midrib. Remove the large midrib with knife or scissors or tear it off. Roll the doubled leaf tightly and eat it as you would celery sticks. The tightly rolled leaf has a crisp texture that makes it quite palatable. We haven't yet followed this method to its logical extreme—spreading the leaf with cream cheese or other tasty spread before rolling—but it's sure to happen sooner or later.

It's easy to see how a cult of sorts has grown up around comfrey. The few serious studies on it show an amazingly high protein content (21 to 33 percent). It is considered a good source of minerals too, as well as of vitamins A and C, since the deep-ranging root reaches far to pick up what the plant needs. Comfrey's ancient name of "knit-

37

bone" refers to its fabled healing qualities—due in large part, probably, to its content of allantoin, a known healing agent responsible for granulation, the formation of new tissue after an injury.

Comfrey is a member of the borage family—an attractive, strong perennial with somewhat hairy leaves twelve to eighteen inches long, rising on short stems from a central crown. The flower is a pretty blue bell, fading to pink. We don't wait to see the blossoms, however, because the foliage is at its best if cut before blossoming time. The plant reaches a height of two feet and gets to be as much as a yard across but, since comfrey doesn't throw out creeping roots and hardly ever sets seed, it is remarkably non-invasive for such a sturdy being. It is persistent, returning each year without fail, but it does not spread. Comfrey stays where it's planted.

You can plant comfrey—roots or plants—at any time during the year, as long as the ground can be worked. We recommend planting comfrey in its own separate plot or bed. Root cuttings are by far the best choice. They start more slowly than the more expensive crown cuttings or whole plants, but they soon catch up. Within a year, you won't be able to tell which was which. Bury each unpromising-looking finger of root horizontally at a depth of three to six inches and space them three feet apart each way. When the comfrey really catches on, you'll understand the reason for that generous spacing. If your ship-ment of roots includes some tiny, hopeless-looking nubbins, plant those too! We've raised some good plants from the "crumbs" left at the bottom of the shipping carton.

We cut continuously from our plants all season long—from April or May till November. Our plot of forty plants is protected with a mulch which helps to retard weeds and keeps the leaves clean. Winter hardy to minus forty degrees, comfrey is not bothered by any insects or disease. Our local herb specialist tells me that comfrey makes a superb houseplant—one from which, like chives, you can cut at will all winter.

CORN

Zea mays saccharata

Sure, you can buy corn at the store, and sometimes at farm stands, too. But the corn you grow yourself is a whole 'nother vegetable. Home-grown corn is sweeter and more flavorful than purchased corn for two reasons: you have a choice of seed varieties developed for their flavor rather than their cosmetic appeal when heaped in a bin; and you can eat the corn within a few minutes of picking.

Any corn is at its best only minutes from the patch. That is the reason for the traditional cooking instructions for corn: put the kettle

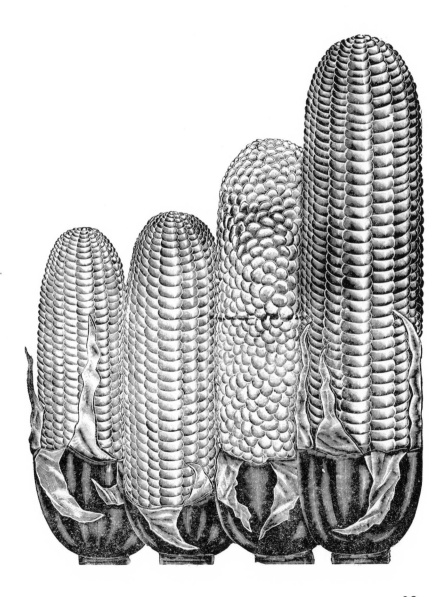

on to boil, *then* go out and pick the ears. To boil water on a wood stove, especially in summer when the fire would be built up just for cooking the corn, would probably require just about that amount of time. We compromise a bit here though; we *steam* our corn, rather than immersing it in boiling water, and the small amount of water we use comes quickly to a boil while we husk the corn.

The minute an ear of corn is picked, its sugar starts to turn to starch. The greatest loss of sweetness occurs in the first twenty-four hours after picking. If you must hold corn, leave the husk on the ear and chill it immediately. Removal of the husk hastens the conversion of sugar to starch.

Varieties to grow:

BUTTER AND SUGAR—one of the sweetest, most tender kinds of corn you can find anywhere. Well named, we think—a favorite with us. Yellow and white kernels.

WONDERFUL—excellent quality in a long, thin ear; sometimes irregularly filled, but delicious. Long harvest period. A midseason corn. The thin ear is deceptive; they are ready before they appear to be.

SILVER QUEEN—said by many to be the sweetest white corn. It *is* the sweetest we've tasted, and the full ears are handsome. Well-protected by husks, they keep well on the stalk for seven to ten days. A late corn.

COUNTRY GENTLEMAN—an open-pollinated, late, white sweet corn. The deep, narrow "shoe peg" kernels are not arranged in rows. In use about 100 years and still a dependable favorite.

GOLDEN BANTAM—another open-pollinated classic. This was one of the first sweet yellow corns introduced. Hard to beat for quality and vitamin content.

ILLINI EXTRA SWEET—This hybrid variety is said to be twice as sweet as others at harvest, and unlike other sweet corn, its sugar turns to starch at a relatively slow rate. For many gardeners, though, it doesn't reach its full potential because pollination by other varieties results in loss of sweetness. It must be widely separated from other corn varieties (at least 200 yards) to reach its genetic potential for super sweetness. A tempting variety, but not the best choice for the average backyard garden unless you grow only this kind and have an agreement with the neighbors!

HONEY AND CREAM—how can you resist a corn with a name like that? Another of the sweet bicolors, this one has a long tight husk that discourages earworm and other insect predation. Quality holds well in the patch. Early midseason.

Corn can be safely planted about the time of the last expected spring

40

frost. Many gardeners gamble on an extra-early planting. If the seed takes, they feast early on corn; if not, little is lost. Early, midseason and late varieties may be planted at the same time.

With a little planning, you can manage a continuous harvest of corn throughout most of the summer, since varieties have been developed to yield extra early, early midseason, midseason and late. (For extra late, just make another planting in early midseason.) We have not always felt that the extra early corn was worth knocking ourselves out for. It depends on how hungry you are for fresh corn, though. We prefer to wait for the full-flavored midseason varieties that evoke sighs of contentment around the table.

Corn is wind-pollinated, so it should be planted in blocks rather than in long single rows. The corn silk strands originate in embryo kernels on the cob; each silk must receive a pollen grain in order for its kernel to develop. When weather is rainy or insect infestation severe, the corn cobs may be incompletely or irregularly filled.

You've probably noticed how vigorously good corn grows. It needs plenty of nitrogen to put out all that leafy growth, so pile on the manure, blood meal or diluted fish fertilizer. We thin the young plants to stand a foot apart in rows two and one-half to three feet apart.

Corn delights in warm, well-drained soil. Keep weeds down by hoeing or tilling until the corn is well over knee high and can hold its own. Don't remove the suckers that may branch out from the base of the plant. They're not superfluous. Although their function isn't completely understood, experienced gardeners and plant experts agree the suckers may help create nourishment for the fast-growing corn plant.

Corn needs plenty of moisture too, especially during the tasselling stage. Notice how effectively the large leaves funnel moisture right down the stalk and on to the roots. In a small plot, you could mulch or irrigate to assure your corn of needed moisture at the right time. We don't, though; once we've manured, planted, thinned and weeded the corn as well as we know how, we simply take our chances. Sometimes there just isn't time during the summer to do all that *could* be done for the garden!

Harvesting time for corn is more critical than for many other vegetables. It is at its best in the milk stage, when the sweet but watery juice in the kernels has turned milky and the kernels are plump but not yet overstuffed.

Most gardeners find that a few ears escape them from time to time and become doughy. This corn needn't be a loss, though; while not fit for eating on the cob, it makes very acceptable corn pudding, soup or fritters.

41

CUCUMBERS

Cucumis sativus

One of the unique pleasures of gardening is the ability to satisfy the special whims of family and friends. So we grow burpless cucumbers for certain special people who find the regular kind a bit hard to take. Most seed dealers carry at least one variety of this non-offending cuke. Each year brings new developments in the burpless line. Sweet Slice is free of bitterness and very disease resistant—a good one to plant if you're troubled by the disease-carrying yellow and black striped cucumber beetle. Burpless is a long, slim Japanese hybrid that is true to its name.

There are other special cucumbers too, that can be yours for a packet of seed. How else would you ever get cukes like these?

LEMON—named for its resemblance, in form and color, to a large lemon, and grown for its good flavor. Try scooping out the seeds and stuffing it!

ORIENTAL CUCUMBERS—for straight fruit from these long, thin Oriental varieties, give the vines a fence or rope netting to climb on, or you'll have cukes shaped like horseshoes.

Sooyow has fine quality, very few seeds.

Kaga is like Sooyow but shorter and smoother, very early.

Kyoto (also listed as China), grows about fifteen inches long, two inches thick, is crisp, thin skinned, milk and mosaic resistant.

GOOD PICKLING VARIETIES . . .

Gherkin, the hedgehog cuke from India, is an oval fruit about two to three inches long and one to one and one-half inches thick, bearing many short, fleshy spines. Grown for their fine flavor when pickled. Good for relishes too. Pick them while young and tender.

Pioneer (fifty-one days) is a heavy-yielding gynoecious (producing only female blossoms) hybrid with good disease tolerance. Produces fewer funny-shaped cukes than other gynoecious hybrids.

Patio-Pick is a compact plant, very early (forty-eight days), producing pickling cucumbers that can be sliced for salads when fully developed.

Cucumbers thrive on warm, rich, loose, well-drained soil. There's no point in planting cukes before the soil warms up and frost danger has passed, unless you want to start a few plants in peat pots indoors to get a jump on the season. I've never been able to decide whether this is worth doing . . . well, perhaps I have, in a way, since I don't do it any more. You may want to try some, though. The seedlings are appealingly vigorous and starting a few is good therapy for spring fever.

When weather is mild and fairly settled, about the time that late iris are in bloom, we plant about eight seeds to a hill, thinning later to four plants. Hills are spaced about five feet apart. To plant cucumbers in rows, grow them a foot apart in rows six feet apart.

We dust around the plants with wood ashes to help repel the cucumber beetle. Our most successful protection ploy has been to plant a ring of radishes around each hill of cucumbers. We've enjoyed much larger cucumber harvests since we started to do this. The radishes don't give total control, but we do get a crop, which is what counts. Hand-picking the beetles early in the season helps to cut down on season-long damage too. We always plant a mildew- and mosaic-resistant variety for added insurance against insect-borne diseases and make an early summer planting to take over if the first planting does succumb to mildew or wilt.

A period of drought can make each cucumber developing at that time unpleasantly bitter. New cukes formed after adequate rain or irrigation will be good. I pickled some of the bitter ones last year and found that the bitterness seemed to have vanished in the pickling process.

Unless you've chosen to plant seed of a gynoecious cucumber (one, like Pioneer, that produces only female blossoms), not all of the blossoms will form fruit. The male blossoms open first, followed in a week or so by the female blossoms, which will bear fruit when polli-

43

nated. The gynoecious hybrids, bearing all-female blossoms, set a heavy crop of fruit. (A pollen carrier to insure fertilization is included in the seed packet.) They do, however, have a tendency to set more misshapen fruit.

In June, when the soil has warmed, we spread a thick hay mulch around the growing vines. Cucumbers need good drainage, plenty of moisture and abundant organic matter in the soil. We find that we can fertilize them efficiently, using the hill system, by burying compost or well-rotted manure in the hole before planting.

Once you've seen the plants past the early stages, the blossoms and cucumbers will come on fast. Most domestic cucumbers take only fifty to sixty days to bear. The Oriental varieties are a little slower, bearing at around seventy-five days. Soon you will be proudly harvesting cukes . . . slicing crisp rounds into your daily salad, filling a pickle crock, and making it possible for your relatives and friends to enjoy a treat they would otherwise miss.

ENDIVE, ESCAROLE

Cichorium endivia

The names of these plants are not interchangeable, as you might think from common usage. Endive has curled, deeply cut or fringed leaves. Escarole, sometimes listed in catalogues as Batavian endive, has broad, flat leaves and a somewhat milder flavor, though both greens are agreeably pungent.

Many gardeners blanch endive and escarole to achieve a milder flavor. The pale, tender hearts have less Vitamin A than the deep green, slightly bitter leaves. The easiest way to blanch the heads is to tie the outer leaves up over the heart of the plant with a soft, strong cloth. Be sure to do this when the leaves are dry, or the heart may rot. As you tie up the leaves, flick out and destroy any slugs that might be on them.

It took us several years of growing endive, ending with a trial planting of escarole in the fall, to decide that we prefer the milder, more buttery heads of escarole. We also have the best luck with it in the fall, since it is difficult to plant these two early enough in the spring so that they can mature before hot weather intensifies their natural good bitterness beyond acceptability.

For spring greens, we depend on loose leaf lettuce, since it is ready

44

in roughly half the time needed to bring escarole to the table. But for fall greens, the well-blanched heads of escarole hold their quality well in the lingering cool days. If well protected by mulch, they easily weather light frosts and often real freezes. If good solid heads are still growing in the row when killing frost is expected, the heads may be dug and grown on in a box of soil in a cool, moist cellar.

Endive and escarole are somewhat less sensitive to cold than lettuce is, but their growing requirements are the same: plenty of moisture, good drainage, generous nitrogen and a steady supply of humus in the soil. Seed may be sown in the open row and thinned, but we find that in both the spring (when you need a head start to beat the hot weather), and summer (when hot, dry soil can be inhospitable to all but summer weed seeds), the best plan is to raise a flat of seedlings and set them out at twelve-inch intervals in the row. Or you can spot the seedlings here and there in the garden where there may be gaps in the rows of other plantings. Plants set out in August will form luscious big rosettes of leaves by October.

In hot summers, both endive and escarole will bolt to seed. When they do, you can see in the blue flower and the leaves of the upper stalk the plant's resemblance to its close relative, chicory.

Escarole and endive are usually served as salad greens but they are also good braised and topped with butter or grated cheese. The more bitter but highly nutritious green outer leaves are good cooked in soup or with other mild greens like comfrey.

FENNEL *or* FINNOCHIO
Foeniculum vulgare dulce

Fennel is one of those vegetables that can make the difference between an ordinary meal and a memorable one. We like it braised, especially with fish, but it is equally tasty sliced in salads, or steamed and served in cream sauce. It is especially good with mixed rice dishes. In addition, it is one of a very few vegetables that are good to eat bulb, stalk, stem, leaves, seeds and all. We mince the tiny, feathery thinnings

into salads, cook the bulb and stem, serve the crisp stalk as we would celery, and munch on the aromatic seeds.

I've occasionally seen fennel sold at the 9th Street pushcart market in South Philadelphia, but never at a standard store. It is so good and so versatile that it's hard to understand why it hasn't caught on more widely. Never mind, though—you can grow your own so easily!

When buying seed, choose the variety *Foeniculum vulgare dulce*. (*F. vulgare*, from which *F. vulgare dulce* was probably developed, is grown mainly for its aromatic foliage and seeds, not the basal bulb. It is properly called sweet fennel and is usually listed with the herbs in seed catalogues.) The bulbing variety grown for vegetable use is commonly referred to as Florence fennel or Finocchio; when listed, it is among the vegetables. It has a thickened base of overlapping stems and a shorter stem than sweet fennel. Both plants are similar in form and habit to dill, though somewhat larger and slightly more frost-tender.

Sow fennel seed in spring when the ground has begun to warm up a bit, but before the last frost. You can make repeated small plantings— the best way to assure a continuous supply of fennel stalks at just the right stage of crispness. The last planting in summer will yield a fall crop that will withstand light frosts. Thin the plants to stand ten inches apart in the row, in rows about eighteen inches apart. The bulbous stalk matures about ninety days after planting, but the plant may be used at any time, even if not full grown. When the basal bulb begins to look as though it's going to amount to something, many gardeners blanch it by drawing up loose earth around the plant. This step is not necessary, though.

Fennel has been entirely free of both disease and insect problems in our experience. Possibly its aromatic foliage repels insect attack. At any rate, it's nice to have a few vegetables around that can fend for themselves as fennel can.

JERUSALEM ARTICHOKE
Helianthus tuberosus

This native American plant—a member of the sunflower family— is one of the most independent and dependable vegetables you can grow. It is not subject to any disease or insect that I can discover; certainly our own planting has been trouble-free. A perennial, it multiplies rapidly, survives severe winters, and stores well right where it grows, as long as the ground can be kept soft enough for digging. The edible portion is a knobby tuber which contains no starch. Its carbohydrate is in the form of inulin and levulan, readily metabolized as the natural sugar levulose. For this reason, the vegetable is of special interest to diabetics, who are usually able to tolerate carbohydrates in this form.

The Jerusalem artichokes grown in gardens today are just like those that the Indians grew and ate centuries ago. While scattered gardeners may have practiced selection of individual strains, no concerted effort has been made to alter the plant as a whole. Certainly its vigor, pest-resistance and ability to hold its own against weedy competition couldn't be improved upon. Even poor soil doesn't discourage what the Indians called the "sun root." All these virtues . . . and it even tastes good!

The flavor of the tubers might best be described as nut-like; the texture is delightfully crisp. Our family enjoys eating the vegetable as a crunchy finger food, grated or cut in salads. Sliced, briefly steamed and mixed with sprouts, sugar peas, peppers and other vegetables, they give the texture of water chestnuts to Chinese-style dishes. You needn't peel the tubers before serving—just scrub them with a brush and cut out creases that might harbor grit.

Since the sun root seldom if ever produces seed, it is propagated by digging up and dividing the tubers. Several mail-order nurseries sell the tubers, or you may find that putting a want-ad in your local paper will bring you calls from nearby gardeners who can spare you a start.

Choose your planting site well. Jerusalem artichokes are not only perennial—they are rapid and enthusiastic multipliers! Gardeners who have made the mistake of planting a row of the tubers in their vegetable patches call them invasive . . . or worse! That's just the nature of the plant. They're well worth growing, so just give them a place by themselves—along a fence, by the garage, next to a shed or around the compost pile.

Cut the seed tubers into two or three sections, each one having an "eye" or incipient bud. Plant the pieces four inches deep, about two feet apart. The unbranched stalk grows to a height of six to nine feet, topped in late summer by a daisy-sized yellow flower. The tubers start to form in August and may be harvested after the flowers fall. Many people wait to dig Jerusalem artichokes until after a hard frost, when the roots are supposedly even more flavorful. We've dug tubers before frost too, and they tasted very good to us.

When you do unearth the tubers, take up no more than you'll use in two to three weeks. The sun root has a very thin skin that doesn't toughen into a protective coating the way a potato skin does. Even in the refrigerator, the tubers will shrivel and spoil within a few weeks. They keep well in damp sand, but the best plan is to protect the plants with a heavy mulch before the ground freezes hard, and then keep digging at intervals for as long as you can. You can resume digging up tubers for a month or so in early spring once the ground can be worked.

Although its tubers do seem to grow larger in friable soil, the Jerusalem artichoke will thrive in poor soil if given a moderate supply of potassium in order to form its carbohydrate-rich root. We find that a shovelful of wood ashes thrown on the ground around the plants once or twice a year supplies all the potassium (potash) they need. Avoid piling on nitrogenous fertilizers, though; too much nitrogen results in large top growth and small tubers. If they fail anywhere, it is likely to be in the very hot or dry parts of the extreme South and West. Otherwise they are pretty much a national vegetable—a good one to get to know better.

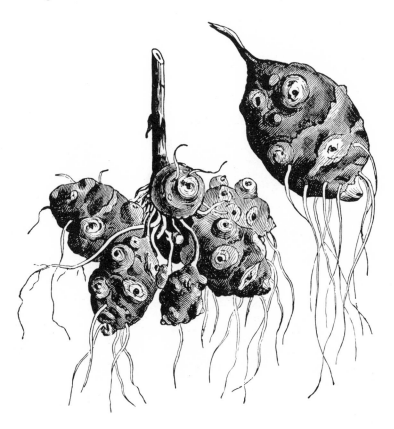

KALE

Brassica oleracea acephala

Another super-vegetable that should be more widely grown is this leafy member of the cabbage family. Resistant to insects and disease, hardy even in the far north, very rich in vitamins and minerals, kale can extend your fresh-vegetable season well into the winter. Like most other green leafy vegetables, kale thrives on rich soil and makes its best growth of tender, mild leaves in cool weather.

For a spring crop, plant the seed as soon as the soil can be worked. The leaves will be ready to harvest within two months of planting. In hot weather, kale tends to be tough and inferior in flavor, but the plant will be usable again when cool fall weather begins.

We find that we are most grateful for kale in the fall—when wood-splitting and leaf-raking have sharpened our appetites for steaming bowls of kale soup or mounds of fresh-cooked greens served with

the first new sausage of the season. To have kale ready to pick by frost, we must remember in midsummer (about ten to twelve weeks before the first frost) how much we enjoyed it the previous year, and find a place in the garden where we can sow the seeds in rows about eighteen to twenty-four inches apart. The four-inch-high seedlings should be thinned to stand about twelve inches apart in the row. We like these tender young thinnings cooked in soup.

When tomato vines lie shrivelled by frost, flowers no longer bloom, the trees are leafless, and even the parsley in the cold frame hugs the ground, then kale comes into its own. Frost has mellowed its flavor. The fringy-curled leaves are still green, still vigorous. Kale is, in fact, a beautiful plant. When you pick those tender inner leaves for your dinner, bring in a few of the fabulously curled and fringed outer leaves for a centerpiece arrangement.

When night temperatures begin to dip regularly into the mid twenties, it is time to protect your kale so you can continue to harvest it all winter. Tuck some straw, old cornstalks or spoiled hay around and partly over it. Many northern gardeners pick kale from under the snow during the winter. Where winters are mild, kale will live until spring without protection.

All that exuberant leafy growth requires a good supply of nitrogen. We plant kale in well-manured soil and give it several doses of manure tea during the growing season.

KOHLRABI

Brassica caulorapa

If you were to go looking for a kohlrabi to buy, you might find it something of a challenge to describe: a solid, round greenish-white vegetable that grows above the ground, with broccoli-like leaves rising directly from the "bulb." Chances are that it wouldn't be on the produce counter, anyway. Kohlrabi's reputation has probably suffered, over the years, from the reluctance of gardeners to pick it young enough.

To appreciate its mild flavor and crisp texture at its best, start plucking your kohlrabi when it reaches a diameter of two inches. It is delicious sliced into salads or served as a crunchy relish with a cheese or onion dip. We prize it especially because it provides a crisp touch to our early leaf-lettuce salads before the cucumbers are ready. Kohlrabi leaves are edible too. Larger kohlrabi, up to tennis-ball size, are good cooked in slices or cubes. I often include strips of cooked kohl-rabi in canned mixed-vegetable pickles. Very large kohlrabi, softball size or so, tend to be woody unless they have grown very rapidly in a cool, wet spring.

Since kohlrabi matures fast (forty-four to sixty days), takes little room and does well in cold weather, it is an ideal spring vegetable for gardeners in cold climates. You can plant the seed about the time you'd plant beets . . . a week or so after the ground has first dried enough to be worked. It is best grown as a fall crop in the southern states, where it can often survive the winter.

The two varieties of kohlrabi most commonly listed are Early White

Vienna and the later Purple Vienna. Kohlrabi Prague Special produces very early crops of tender bulbs, but only one seed dealer that I can find carries it. The seed seems to germinate at least 100 percent, like that of cabbage. Thin the plants to stand five inches apart in rows fifteen to eighteen inches apart. The only insect that has troubled our kohlrabi has been an occasional flea beetle, for which diatomaceous earth is a safe, effective control.

A fairly rich soil with plenty of moisture promotes the rapid growth conducive to good quality in this vegetable. Since it does not hold its quality in the garden row for as long as cabbage or kale, the best plan is to make frequent small sowings. Then you will have a steady supply of tender, delicious kohlrabi. Where else but in your own garden could you ever find them?

LEAF LETTUCE

Lactuca sativa

Of the four kinds of home garden lettuce (head lettuce, leaf lettuce, butterhead and cos or romaine), the leaf and butterhead sorts are the most widely grown . . . with good reason too, for their fine quality and flavor and superior vitamin content make them superb salad ingredients. The tender leaves bruise and wilt so readily that they are too fragile for commercial use.

Leaf lettuce grows in an open, green rosette of frilled leaves. Butterhead lettuce forms a loose, green head in which a few of the inner leaves blanch white. Head lettuce is grown for its crisp, but less nutritious, tightly wrapped blanched leaves. Some old garden books recommend throwing the outer green leaves of lettuce to the chickens and eating only the pale inner leaves. Today we know better; those green leaves, rich in Vitamin A, are the most valuable part of the plant.

Plant lettuce as early in the spring as the ground can be worked, continuing to make small plantings every two weeks until late summer, or six weeks before expected frost. Since leaf lettuce is ready to eat within two months of planting (most loose-leaf varieties take about forty-five days; the butterheads average sixty days) it may be seeded between rows of long-season crops like cauliflower or Brussels sprouts that will later take over. Or it will do well in a row of its own, interplanted with radishes.

Many gardeners sow an early patch of lettuce as a solid block, perhaps in an especially favored early-warming, well-drained spot. You can grow a lot of leaf lettuce that way in a small space. One of the most charming spring gardens I've seen had a patchwork grouping of block-planted lettuce of four or five different kinds. Worth growing for cheering spring green whether you need that much lettuce or not! (Hint: if those tender leaves are really coming on, you can consume more of them as wilted lettuce with a hot sweet/sour vinegar dressing.)

Lettuce seed is fine and easily oversown. Space half-grown plants about four inches apart in rows twelve to fifteen inches apart, and keep thinning until the nearly mature plants stand ten to twelve inches apart in the row. Use the thinnings in salads. Since lettuce has a shallow root system, it transplants easily. For the same reason,

though, it needs a steady supply of moisture to maintain the rapid growth that makes for mildness and good leaf quality. Lettuce is 90 percent water.

Slugs like lettuce, but they seldom pose a serious threat. If the slugs in your garden do start to gang up on your lettuce, trap them under boards or in shallow saucers of water with yeast dissolved in it. I find that with slugs, as with other insect pests, my sense of outrage banishes squeamishness. If I'm upset enough about the damage they're doing, I find it easy to hand-pick and crush them.

Lettuce likes rich soil. Ground that has been well manured and limed is ideal. For a boost, try side dressings of blood meal or diluted fish emulsion. A mulch helps to keep roots cool and moisture in and protects the good outer leaves from rain-splashed mud.

All varieties of lettuce are at their best during the cooler months. Midsummer heat causes most kinds to bolt to seed, rather than head. Some kinds stand summer heat quite well, though, especially Butter-crunch, a loose-heading, crisp, green butterhead type of superb quality. We grow it all summer, picking our best heads from plant-ings that grow in the shade of taller plants. A volunteer pumpkin vine nursed our last year's Buttercrunch through the summer. Matchless and Bibb are also fine butterhead types. Among the loose-leaf vari-eties, Oak Leaf, Resistant and Salad Bowl hold their quality well in warm weather. For fun, grow Tom Thumb, a tiny compact head useful for individual servings. Black Seeded Simpson does well in spring and fall. It's hard to go wrong on lettuce varieties. The only one we haven't liked has been Ruby—not crisp enough for us.

If "lettuce" to you still means a solid, store-bought head, then you have a treat awaiting you!

LEEKS

Allium porrum

If you have a good, flavorful chicken and want to make cock-a-leekie soup, you'll need leeks. No doubt you'll find it easier to grow them than to search the markets.

A hardy biennial, the leek has been grown since prehistory. It is a member of the onion family but forms no bulb. The stalk is the same width as the base, flaring into a series of flat, ribbon-like leaves. Its flavor is milder than onion.

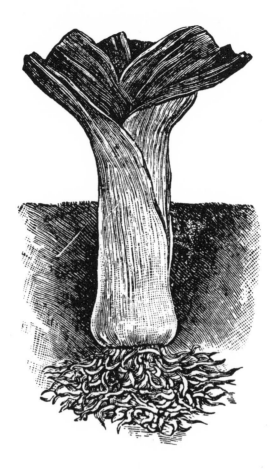

Growing leeks is good tonic for the impatient gardener in winter, for they may be started indoors by planting seed in flats in February or March. Transplant the young three-inch-tall spears into larger flats, about two inches apart. They'll grow another inch or so before it's time to plant them outside—at about the time the apple trees are in bloom. Since leeks require a long growing season (130 days), this method gives you a head start.

You can also plant the seed outdoors when the ground is open and workable in the spring. Set the young plants six inches apart in rows eighteen inches apart. Blanch them by drawing up soil around the base as they grow. You may want to wrap cardboard around each half-grown leek before you hill it up with soil, to prevent particles of soil from being enveloped in the layers of the growing leek. Moist,

56

deeply-dug soil with good drainage, cool weather and plenty of humus help to grow good leeks.

Leeks shouldn't have problems with insect infestation, except perhaps for onion thrips in a dry, hot year. These active little insects pierce cell walls, causing scars and, in severe cases, stunting the plant. Prevent thrip problems before they start by destroying all affected onions rather than leaving them in the rows, and removing weed cover that provides winter protection for the pests.

Although leeks may occupy the garden row for the best part of the growing year, their winter hardiness makes up for it. Well mulched or banked with earth, they survive cold but not severe weather right in the garden row. Most cold-climate gardeners will want to dig at least part of their crop for storage. Keep the plants in a cool, dark place as near forty degrees as possible, with the roots in damp soil or sand.

Unique, Artico, North Pole and Conqueror are good winter-hardy varieties. Musselburgh is adaptable to different conditions. The Lyon is solid with a very fine flavor.

When you dash out to the garden in the gathering winter dusk to pull two wrist-thick leeks for the evening's soup, you'll be glad you planted the seeds way back in the spring. I know I am, and as I sprint—shivering—back to the kitchen, I think: "Next year, more leeks."

OKRA

Hibiscus esculentus

There's no reason why okra can't be grown in most of the United States. It likes warm weather, but since it bears fifty-five to seventy-five days after planting, that shouldn't be too hard to arrange. Any climate where eggplant and cucumbers thrive will be fine for okra too. Warmer areas of the South usually manage to grow two crops of okra in a year.

Okra will grow in any good garden soil; in well-drained, fertile soil it really flourishes. Plant the seeds after the danger of frost is past, when the soil has become thoroughly warm and the air temperature remains fairly steady at above sixty degrees. Make your rows three feet apart, thinning dwarf okra varieties, which grow to a height of three feet, to stand fifteen to eighteen inches apart. The tall varieties that reach up to five feet in height should be spaced two to three feet apart in the row. The larger plants make a good hedge or border. Dwarf varieties fit better into the average home garden.

Okra blooms with a decorative flower that shows its relationship to the ornamental hibiscus. Its botanical name, in fact, means "edible hibiscus." Within a few days after the flowers drop, pods will be ready to pick.

We found out, when we first planted okra, why it is a home gar-

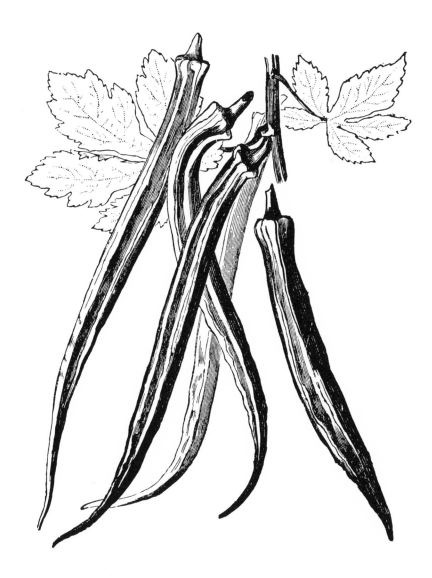

dener's specialty. The pods must be picked at least every other day, preferably daily; otherwise they will turn woody and begin to ripen seed. Once that process starts, the plant figures it is accomplishing its purpose in life (to set seed) and quits producing new pods.

If one day's picking doesn't yield enough pods for a meal, they may be refrigerated for a day or so. Keep them well spread out and slightly moist, though; they stay tender for only a short while after picking.

Okra is good stewed, braised with onion, sliced into soup or breaded and fried.

It is probably best to blanch and freeze those first small pickings for later use in soup. They may also be dried by stringing and hanging in a hot, dark attic. Large pods should be split for drying but small ones may be left whole.

If your okra should start to bear while you're away and you return to a patch of woody, overmature pods, all is not lost. The tender green seeds, before they harden to maturity, may be shelled and cooked like peas. If you really feel adventurous, you might like to try drying and grinding the seed for a coffee substitute.

Perhaps because of the faint fuzzy stickiness of the pod, okra seems to be pretty well immune to insect attack. Cotton bollworm may damage the pods in southern areas. Southern gardeners, of course, can buy okra in food markets, but never as tender, wholesome and fresh as that they can raise themselves. And north of Maryland, it's grow your own or do without!

PARSNIPS

Pastinaca sativa

Parsnips are not grown in home gardens as often as they might be, perhaps because for most people the only taste of the vegetable has come from a cello pack on a store counter. So, few people buy parsnips and few people grow them! Yet, when well grown and well prepared, they have a delicious flavor and a pleasing texture. The only way to discover whether you've been missing a flavor you'd enjoy is to plant a short row of parsnips, be it the fine-grained Hollow Crown Improved or Harris Model, or the earlier All America, tend them well, let the frost nip them for a week or two, and dig them as you need them for as long as the supply lasts. The roots keep extremely well all winter long, needing only a mulch to keep the soil soft enough to dig. Be sure to use your parsnips before they begin to grow new tops in the spring, for they become bitter then.

Let's get those roots planted first, though. They take about 120 days to mature, so you want to get an early start by planting seed in spring, about when daffodils are blooming—not the very first thing in spring, or the seed may rot. Parsnip seed must be fresh; seed more than a year old doesn't germinate well, and even fresh seed should be sown fairly thickly, about one seed every two inches, in rows eighteen to twenty-four inches apart. Cover the seed with no more than one-

quarter inch of soil. Parsnips don't need rich soil, but it should be as loose and deeply dug as possible since those roots really go delving. Germination is slow—two or three weeks. Some gardeners sow radish seed along with the parsnip seed, to break the ground first for the young parsnips. The seedlings resemble those of celery, with a broadly fringed leaf. They grow very slowly. You have to look carefully for what seems like months to avoid stepping on them. But when they do form good tops, they grow steadily even after a frost and should be thinned to stand four to six inches apart. Parsnips have no serious pests in our area; in some localities they may be subject to the same insects that prey on carrots: carrot rust fly and wire worm. The roots themselves may become forked in heavy clay soil, if hoeing is done too close to the plant, or if fresh manure is applied to the row. In very sandy soil, the plants produce many extra root fibers. Parsnips are easier to prepare for the table when the root is long, thick and un-branched. Forked roots are perfectly good to eat but they are a nuisance to clean and chop and more of the vegetable is likely to be wasted.

When ready to harvest, after several weeks of frost have changed much of the starch in the roots to sugar, the parsnips should be dug, never pulled. They will probably measure about three inches across at the top, and may be a good foot long—a lot of vegetable. A fifty-foot row will yield about a bushel, certainly plenty for the average family.

Parsnips shrivel if dug and exposed to the air, even in a damp root cellar. If your winters are too severe to permit January digging, you can heap your parsnips in a cold but not freezing place, well covered with moist soil.

Gardeners who live where winters are very mild sometimes en-counter another problem. Those persistent parsnips, already in the ground since spring, keep on growing throughout the winter, getting woodier every day. The solution here is to go along with the parsnips' way of doing things and make a fall planting which can mature slowly during the cold but not frigid winter months.

Cooking methods have a lot to do with the acceptability of parsnip dishes. Since the natural sweetness of the vegetable is readily dissolved by cooking in water, or even steaming, the best ways to retain and accentuate the really delightful flavor of a good parsnip are to sauté it in oil, bake it as you would a potato, cut it into rounds and bake it with butter in a casserole, or French fry it. In all cases, keep heat low to avoid scorching the sugar in the vegetable. Parsnips with lamb and peas is our idea of a good meal to come home to on a cold day. We look around the table, noting how much of the meal has come from our own ground, and we are content.

61

PEAS

Pisum sativum

Green peas start to lose quality within two hours after picking, when their natural sugars begin to turn to starch. Is it any wonder, then, that even the most ordinary garden pea, fresh-picked, is a better food than any you could buy?

Among the peas there are some very special sorts. Any home gardener who has two months of good cool spring growing weather can raise peas for some fine early summer eating. For successive crops, plant seed of early and late maturing varieties on the same day. We like Marvel (early) and Lincoln (main crop) for regular garden peas. We try others, and I'm sure we're missing still other good kinds, but we seem to come back to these.

For truly splendid flavor, try the French Petit Pois, a small but delicious and highly productive pea.

If your summers come on early, hot and dry, or if you've not found it possible to plant pea seed early enough (as in some community gardens where the soil is plowed late), you'll be glad for Wando, a dependable cropper even in warm weather. The quality can't match that of the cool-grown early varieties, but you'll get peas.

The sugar pea, also called snow pea or edible-pod pea, is a vegetable of superb quality that is easy to raise and simple to prepare. It freezes well and has few calories. The pods are eaten whole while they are still slim, before the peas begin to swell. The flavor is mild, sweet, pea-like and delicious. When properly stir-fried or briefly steamed, the texture is delicately crisp. For a new twist on a favorite traditional menu, try serving sugar peas with your salmon on July 4th.

We plant two varieties of sugar peas: Dwarf Grey Sugar, a low-growing bushy plant with beautiful purple blossoms and peas about two to two and one-half inches long; and Mammoth Melting Sugar, a tall, five-foot climber that bears pods three to four inches long at their best, which is very good indeed. If you choose to grow only the dwarf sugar peas, we recommend Dwarf Grey Sugar over the Dwarf White; the Grey has a much finer flavor. The dwarf plants are ready with their crop a few days before the mammoth, though both are always planted at the same time. The mammoth is our favorite for taste and tenderness. We find, too, that its pods remain in prime condition for up to four days.

Peas are the first outdoor planting we make; our pea seed goes into the ground as early as the soil can be worked. We plant the seed in paired rows four inches apart, the pairs of rows set at intervals of thirty-six inches in the garden.

Inoculating the seed with nitrogen-fixing bacteria before planting ensures that the legume roots will have the bacterial help they need to convert atmospheric nitrogen into a form usable by the next plants to grow in the row. It also encourages a generous yield. If inoculated legumes (peas, beans, limas or soybeans) have been grown in this same space recently, you may not need to inoculate again. The way to determine this is to pull the spent legume plants from the previous

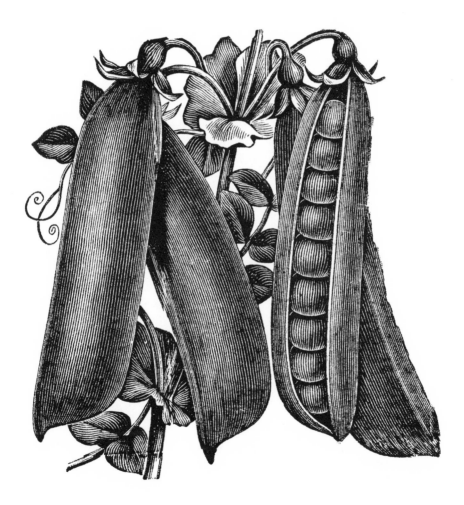

crops. If there are many nodules on the roots, the bacteria are there and doing their job. If root nodules are sparse, it is best to inoculate again—a simple procedure involving an inexpensive packet of powder shaken over the moistened seeds.

We firm the soil gently around each seed, as with other garden plantings, in order to encourage good germination. There is enough moisture in the ground in early spring to foster sprouting if the seed is in good close contact with the soil, so sprinkling the newly planted seed is not necessary.

Sugar peas need support to do their best; in our opinion there is nothing better for this task than brushy branches. Three-foot brush is adequate for the low-growing dwarf peas. For the tall-growing mammoths, we set five-foot brush; next to that we string a network of binder's twine in five rows between steel stakes. We think that the three-dimensional brush exposes more of the plant to light and air, but string netting or chicken-wire fencing make perfectly acceptable substitutes if brush is hard to come by.

Gathering pea brush is an annual ritual for us. Of course, we could save it from year to year, but then we would need another excuse in April to go out along the hedgerow, through the bee yard, and around the upper woods. We often take our goats along on these jaunts, to browse on the greening honeysuckle while we make piles of the brush which we drag down to the garden. Taking an old axe and a plank to the garden's edge, I chop pointed ends on each branch so that it will go deep into the soil.

If you have no source of brush on your place, watch for the tree-trimming crew in spring and fall.

It seems to take more time for the peas to sprout than for the rest of the plant to grow, possibly because we get busier and busier in the garden as spring's arrival becomes imminent. All at once, there are blossoms on the peas, and once the blossoms have appeared, the peas are not far behind.

They may be picked at any time after the pod has formed, until the pea bumps begin to round out. Our first picking is usually a handful of scandalously young, delicious little one- to one-and-a-half-inch pods. All they need is a minute or two of steaming and a dab of butter.

Older peas, either fresh or frozen, are perfect for combining with onions and bean sprouts to make a meal that we, at least, never tire of. We sauté onions in a heavy pan, sometimes with pepper strips, then add the peas and sprouts, possibly with small pieces of cooked chicken or pork, and cover the pan for five minutes of cooking over low heat. We serve this with buttered brown rice, a good soy sauce, and plenty of freshly grated Parmesan cheese.

When the sugar peas are well under way and producing as many as we can pick, we like to make a meal of them: a big earthenware stew plate of freshly picked, briefly cooked buttered peas, with nothing else on the table to detract from their flavor. (Later, after milking, while the fireflies dance over the meadow, we'll sit on the porch with bowls of homemade ice cream. The simple life? Well, yes and no!)

PEPPERS

Capsicum frutescens

The store shopper whose list says "peppers" will most likely add a bag of green bell peppers to the pile in the shopping cart. To a gardener, though, the word "peppers" calls to mind a wide variety of colors, shapes and flavors . . . Bell Boy, Peter Piper and Bell-Ringer—blocky, thick-walled sweet bell peppers that ripen to glossy red in your garden; banana peppers—long, thin, sweet pods ranging as they ripen from pale green to yellow, orange and red; Pimiento peppers—heart shaped, thick walled, and sweet as an apple; Sweet Cherry—diminutive sweet pods, ripening from green to red, just right for pickling and garnishing. And the hots . . . Long Red Cayenne, Yellow Hungarian, Large Red Cherry, Jalapeno, Anaheim, Tabasco—all different shapes and sizes, with potency ranging from hot (Anaheim and Hungarian Wax) to HOT (Jalapeno, Long Red Cayenne, Large Red Cherry, Numex Big Jim).

To get the kind of plants we want, we order seed of several different varieties and start seedlings indoors in January or February. The stocky plants, raised under lights, often have blossoms on them when we set them out in mid-May when the last frost is safely behind us—the same time that we plant out tomato seedlings. We space the plants eighteen to twenty-four inches apart in the row, with rows two to three feet apart, depending on variety.

We like Sweet Banana for its bushy habit and exuberant production —scads of multicolored tapered pods. Children often nickname this the Pinocchio pepper: the long, slim, pointed fruit is just the right size and shape to stand in for the wooden puppet's nose. Our yearly standby for thick-walled sweet bell peppers is the hybrid Bell Boy, an early variety that bears green peppers for us by late June and red ones by early August. Red peppers have twice the Vitamin C content of green ones, but slightly less Vitamin A. There are many other good

65

bell pepper varieties, like Calwonder, Vinedale, Canape and others. The best plan is to try several different kinds and see which one seems to do best in your climate and soil. Calwonder grows well in warm climates but often performs poorly in Northern gardens. Vinedale is a good choice for short growing seasons since it blossoms and bears early.

The sweet cherry pepper that we grow is an un-named kind known to us only as Amelia's peppers, from seed saved and given us by a Lancaster County woman who raises them on her farm. They make a fine jewelled garnish for a bowl of coleslaw. Most of our harvest, though, goes into a pickle that is taken for granted in Pennsylvania but seldom

seen elsewhere. Ream out seeds from cherry peppers. Stuff them with grated cabbage. Arrange them in a jar, including some of each color— red, green, orange. Shake in some celery seed and tuck in a bay leaf. Pour on your favorite sweet-and-sour pickling mixture. (We use one cup of vinegar to one-half cup of honey, diluted with three-quarters cup of water.) To can the pepper pickles, process them in boiling water for ten minutes. In hopes of keeping this good old pepper variety alive, and perhaps even improving it, I've given seed from our own heirloom strain of cherry peppers to two seed companies, Grace's Gardens and Johnny's Seeds (see Sources, page 124). I don't know whether the seed will be offered as a catalogue listing; it must first be evaluated in field trials.

Peppers do well on a fairly light, not-too-rich, well-limed soil. We use Dolomite limestone since it contains the magnesium that peppers need. In magnesium-deficient soils, the plants will bear spotted leaves that drop prematurely and the fruits are likely to sunburn. Hot peppers tolerate a heavy clay soil better than the sweet peppers. Poor aeration typical of slow-draining heavy soils may result in misshapen fruits.

Pepper blossoms sometimes have an annoying way of dropping off when they become too dry, either from drought or hot drying winds. Adding moisture to the soil won't remedy the problem, but misting a few of the affected plants with a fine spray of water twice a day might help the pepper plant to retain enough blossoms to set a crop of fruit.

Insects are not much of a problem with peppers. Other than an infestation of aphids early in the season (which hasn't happened to us—yet), the most serious insect damage is likely to be from the cutworm, whose encircling bite can be rather final. We tried index cards and cans to protect our plants, but they're a nuisance. The quickest, most effective method we've found to cutworm-proof a seedling is to place a short stick or twig right next to the stem, half above and half below the ground, when setting the plant in its hole. To do its damage, the cutworm must surround the stem, but it can't bite through that hard stick.

If any of your plants are doing poorly, check for evidence of one of the following diseases: mosaic, a virus disease, causes mottled, curled, yellowed leaves, and ultimate stunting of the plant. If it's a problem for you, rotate crops, avoid fertilizing the pepper row with tobacco stems, and grow a mosaic-resistant variety like Yolo Wonder B. A fungal growth, anthracnose, causes soft round dark spots. To control it, rotate crops, keep peppers and beans (also subject to anthracnose) separate, grow resistant varieties, and avoid working with the plants when they are wet. On the whole, peppers are not demanding plants. They are slightly less sensitive to cold than tomatoes and thrive in hot weather, fruit ripening steadily all through those baking August days when gardeners weed early and late, but hibernate with a good book during midday.

At the end of the season, we pick baskets full of all kinds of peppers. Since they're good fresh, cooked, pickled and frozen, they don't seem to hang heavy on our hands. We dry the Long Red Cayenne pods by stringing them on heavy thread. They make bright kitchen garlands— symbols of garden bounty that last from one season to another, ready at any time for snipping into chili.

POTATOES

Solanum tuberosum

Potatoes are habitually served, but seldom fully appreciated. There are potatoes and potatoes; some have excellent flavor and texture; others that may ship and keep well are insipid and waxy. If you have enough space, you might like to try growing potatoes in your garden, if for no other reason than the pleasure of stealing a few new potatoes from each hill to go with the summer's fresh peas.

There are many good varieties of seed potatoes available, far more than the few I'll mention here. The best plan is to try a few different kinds and see which is most pleasing to you, grown under your own particular conditions. When possible, buy seed potatoes locally. Some good kinds are available only by mail, though.

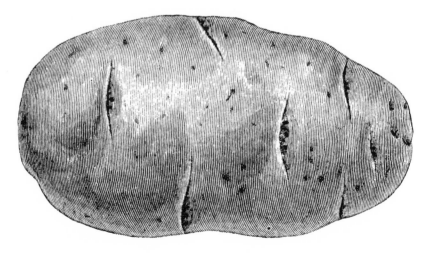

Irish Cobblers have been around for a long time. When well grown, they have an excellent flavor and texture. They tend to have deep-set eyes, but home gardeners can tolerate such traits when quality of the whole potato is good. Cobblers are usually available locally.

The true potato connoisseur may want to try the small fingerling salad potatoes, with yellow flesh and fine flavor. They are especially good for making potato salad, but they fry well too. Cook them without peeling. I doubt whether you'll find these offered outside of the seed catalogues.

Or you may want to try growing a good baking potato, perhaps one of the russets. Norgold Russet is an early potato producing long, smooth, scab-resistant tubers. Shallow-eyed Russet Sebago comes later but yields well. Russet Burbank, a good baker, doesn't always yield heavily, but is usually of excellent quality.

Potato quality and yield depend heavily on the soil in which the crop is grown. Potatoes thrive in acid soil of loose texture. Soil that is not sufficiently acid encourages the development of scab disease. For good, mealy potatoes, make sure the soil has a good supply of potash; greensand and granite dust are good sources.

You can plant potatoes as early in spring as the soil can be worked. We cut each seed potato into pieces, trying for an average of two eyes to the piece and exposing no more cut surface than necessary. We dry our cut pieces for three to four days to let the cut surfaces heal over; they are less likely to rot when dried, especially in heavy soils.

Plant the potato seed eight to twelve inches apart in rows two to three feet apart, and keep soil loose and well hilled around the plant. Or place the seed-potato pieces on a bed of leaves or rotted hay and cover them with more hay, adding further layers as the top growth develops. Potatoes grown in mulch are clean and seldom bothered by the potato beetle, but they form green skins if mulch is insufficient to exclude light. Harvest tubers for storage when the tops have yellowed or died back. Those you want to use as new potatoes may be lifted whenever they are big enough.

PUMPKINS

Cucurbita pepo

Protein from the vegetable garden? It's possible, if you grow one of the new pumpkins that have hull-less seeds. Of course, all pumpkin seeds

are good to eat once you get past that shell. For easy eating, though, you might want to try Lady Godiva, Eat-All or Sweetnut. Each of these varieties has a naked seed which makes a delicious quick snack, salad garnish or side dish with soup and fresh bread. Lady Godiva seeds are large and very tasty. The flesh of the pumpkin is, as the catalogues say, "not of table quality"—it won't hurt you, but it's coarse in texture and flavor. We feed it to our animals. Sweetnut and Eat-All, both of which are technically squashes, have edible flesh—good for pies, especially—and smaller but delicious nutty bare seeds. The seeds of the Sweetnut rank with peanuts as a source of protein and are good either raw or cooked.

Many gardeners with limited space forego pumpkins because they ramble so. But since you can get a double crop—meaty orange flesh and crunchy crisp seeds—from the same plant, these pumpkins do earn the space they occupy. Sweetnut is a good choice for planting in the small patch since it grows in compact bush form. Even Eat-All isn't too rampant; the vines grow only about five feet long. Perhaps you can plant them where they'll shade your summer lettuce. Another semi-bush pumpkin, the new hybrid Funny Face, needs only half the space of a regular pumpkin and bears quantities of medium-sized Hallowe'en pumpkins.

Pumpkins may be grown in either rows or hills, or you can sneak in a few at the edge of the corn patch. Sweetnut, like other bush types, does best in a row. Space hills of three to four plants four feet apart in rows five feet apart. Or plant seed every foot in a row six feet away from adjoining rows and thin to retain the best plants.

Regardless of what your neighbor might have told you about having raised a "cucer-kin" or a "watercumber," pumpkins will *not* cross with cucumbers, watermelons or cantaloupes. They *will* cross among themselves, though, and with some gourds and summer and winter squashes. Any crossing that does occur will not show up in the pumpkins and squash you plant this year. It will be evident only in the vegetables raised from seed of this year's crop. So if you've worried, as many gardeners have, about raising pumpkins, cucumbers and melons in the same patch, you can relax. They won't cross. There is no need to worry about growing zucchini and pumpkins next to each other either, as long as you don't count on saving their seed for next year's crop.

Like other cucurbits (squash and cucumbers), pumpkins can be host to some annoying insects. The same remedies apply; see the sections on cucumbers and squash.

Pumpkins do take space, it's true—space that, in a tiny garden, could (and should) be used to grow much more food. But, if you can find an odd corner for a bush or vine, you'll have pumpkins to pile by your front step in the fall, and plenty of crisp seeds to snack on.

RADISHES

Raphanus sativus

If you want to grow a good radish that is solid, crisp, tangy but not bitter—one that holds its quality for weeks while continuing to grow—try our favorite, China Rose. This is a fall radish (sometimes called a winter keeper) that we plant in August for harvesting from October on. It is smooth skinned, with a lovely subtle rose color, and measures four to six inches long and about two inches across. China Rose stands a pretty hard freeze and keeps well in the row under mulch or in moist sand in basement or cold-cellar storage. We've found that an easy way to get this crop in the ground is to scatter the seeds in the shallow trench left when we pull onions in August. We cover the radish seeds firmly with loose soil and try to keep the area shaded and moist for a week or so until they germinate. We usually forget about them during the busy harvesting and processing days of September, but there comes a day in early October when I have a moment to linger in the garden on my way from the barn . . . and there is the first fall radish! Its light crispness is the perfect complement to the hearty fare that starts to appear on our table once the days of cold soup-and-salad meals are over.

Other good long-standing radishes include Black Spanish and Miyashige, often used in Japan for pickling. Another Oriental radish, Sakurajima, grows to prodigious size without turning pithy. You may want to try the Oriental custom of cooking these crisp, solid radishes, especially in soups.

Plant the winter radishes in late July or early August, thinning them to stand four inches apart in rows about a foot apart. We spread wood ashes in the row to control the radish maggot, which eats tunnels in the roots. In our experience, though, the late plantings have not been infested with this pest as have some of our early spring radish crops. If the root maggot troubles you, be sure to plant your radish seed in ground that has not grown cabbage for three years.

Among the spring radishes, our favorites are Cherry Belle, Short-

Top Scarlet Globe, French Breakfast and Icicle. Early planting and fast growth make for good radishes. Make small, frequent plantings of spring radishes, until hot weather, when they will toughen and go to seed no matter what you do. Spring radishes of good quality are not as easy to grow as rumor would have it. The winter radishes are more dependable producers of excellent food in quantity. In any case, a well-grown radish is not to be belittled. You have a right to be proud of the good radishes your garden grows!

ROOTED PARSLEY

Petroselinum radicatum

For a comforting midwinter soup, we like rounds of this long, white, slender, carrot-like root cooked with chicken broth or in a milk base with onions and fresh snipped chives. The pungent, cut-fringed, but not curled, green tops, rich in Vitamin A, may be used in the same way as regular parsley.

It is for the root that most people grow this vegetable, though. Most seed catalogues carry the variety Hamburg, which is what we have grown. Record, reputed to be larger than Hamburg, is also available, but we haven't grown it yet.

Rooted parsley is an old European favorite unknown to many gardeners, let alone produce department managers. We came across it in our search for a root vegetable that would duplicate the flavor of a soup that my husband Mike enjoyed during a stay in Holland. We're still not sure whether the original vegetable was this one, or perhaps celeriac, but we're happy to have discovered that the rooted form of parsley is worth growing.

Plant seed for rooted parsley as early in the spring as the ground can be worked. Soaking the seed overnight encourages quicker germination, which is at best very slow, as it is in other parsley varieties. It may take a month. Don't give up! It is a good idea, though, to sow a few radish seeds to mark the row so that you don't do as I have done and plant something else there. Keep the area free of weeds so that the young seedlings have the best possible chance. Thin the three-inch-high seedlings to stand one-half inch apart. A later thinning should be made too, so that the developing roots stand one and one-half to two inches apart in the row. Space rows about fifteen inches apart.

73

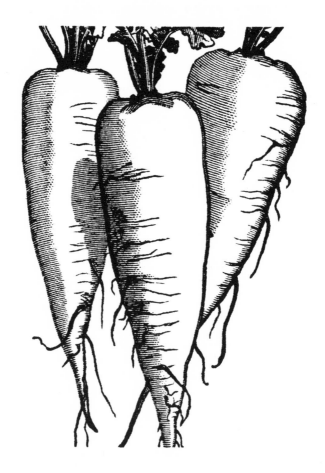

Roots are ready to pull within three months after planting, but they keep well for winter eating either in the ground under mulch or in a damp root cellar or vegetable storage barrel.

SALSIFY *or* OYSTER PLANT
Tragopogon porrifolius

Much to the amusement (and occasional consternation) of my family, I sometimes drive through alleys in towns, especially small

74

towns. I like to see what people are growing in their vegetable patches. Back yards, I think, are much more interesting than front yards. When I see a row of round-headed, complacent-looking cabbages, or endive bunched up and tied, or a row of thin green salsify leaves banked up for winter when the rest of the world is shivering, then I feel a sense of kinship with the people who live there. That gardener knows what's good.

Salsify is a hardy root, slender, thinner than the parsnip, and longer and less tapering than most carrots. Its foliage resembles wide flat blades of grass in a clump. If you've ever grown garlic, you may notice as we have that your salsify plants look like great big enthusiastic clumps of garlic.

When planting salsify, use only seed packed for the current year, since it doesn't stay viable for very long. Mammoth Sandwich Island is the variety to buy (since that's the only one listed in the catalogues!). Sow rows about fifteen inches apart in early spring; daffodil bloom is a good time. Plant the seed rather thickly and thin the seedlings to stand four inches apart in the row. Avoid putting fresh manure around the plants if you don't want forked roots. Your crop will be ready in about 115 days. That's a long time in the garden row, but salsify stays put, doesn't invade other plants, and resists insect attack, so it's no trouble to have around. At the end of the growing season, we're glad we devoted a row to salsify because it is even better flavored after frost and stays in good condition right in the garden, ready to eat for as long as the ground will admit a digging fork. We extend that period by protecting the row with old hay, leaves and cornstalks.

The mature roots are eight inches long and one and one-half inches wide, lovely creamy white. They should always be dug rather than pulled since the tap root grows deep. The roots shrivel when exposed to the air a day or so after they're removed from the ground. For this reason, oyster plant is strictly a home garden vegetable. Any roots you've dug that won't be used right away should be stored in moist sand or sawdust in a cool place.

Why is salsify called the vegetable oyster? Try shredding several of these roots, mixing in an egg and a trace of flour, and frying patties of the mixture in oil. See if that elusive seafood flavor doesn't come through to fool you. Or make a rich milk-base soup with onions and parsley and chopped salsify . . . the gardening gourmet's oyster stew! Salsify is also good served au gratin or steamed and then fried and served with lemon wedges. When preparing salsify, just scrub the roots with a vegetable brush—removing the skin wastes food value and flavor.

The salsify you've kept in the ground all winter under protection

75

will give you yet another dividend in the spring, when it starts to send up new flower stalks. If you pick these shoots while they're still tender and steam them for about twenty minutes, you'll have an early green asparagus-like vegetable that could completely convince you to start another row of salsify.

SORREL

Rumex acetosa

If you've ever raved over a perfect bowl of French sorrel soup, you'll be glad to hear that seed for garden sorrel is available, though uncommon.

A hardy, leafy perennial related to buckwheat, sorrel is a widely adaptable plant that will thrive on ordinary, even poor soil. In well-drained soil of good fertility, it will respond with extra vigor. The long, thin, arrow-shaped leaves are ready to harvest within sixty days of planting. Where summers are extremely hot, the plant slows its production of tender new growth, but resumes growth during cooler early fall days. A well-protected plant will not only live over winter but, in a favorable southeast exposure, may even produce a few new leaves for plucking during a January thaw. The root is deep and tremendously strong. Keep the plant well mulched to retain the moisture it needs for tender growth. Removing the seedstalk in summer will also assure a higher quality leaf.

If you just can't wait for that first taste of cream of sorrel soup, you can get a head start by sowing seeds indoors in flats and planting the seedlings six to eight inches apart in rows about fifteen inches apart. Although a few frosty nights won't hurt the young plants, it's best to wait two to three weeks after planting your first radishes and lettuce to let the weather settle and the soil warm up a bit. Planting seed in the cold frame or the garden row is easier.

Since sorrel is a perennial, the best place for it is in a special perennial vegetable bed along with asparagus, comfrey, rhubarb and horseradish, or in a separate bed of its own. Sorrel takes little room, and a few plants will supply the needs of most families, so a small separate sorrel bed next to a garage or shed would most likely yield all you can use.

Like most leafy deep-green vegetables (perhaps the most neglected food group in our fast-food culture), sorrel is an excellent source of Vitamins A and C, as well as the minerals mined by that deep root. The subtle acid piquancy of fresh sorrel leaves make it a perfect choice for mixing with milder greens like comfrey and chard. A dish of plain cooked sorrel might be a bit tangy for most tastes, especially if American garden sorrel is used. The French sorrel is the mildest known strain. The variety Belleville is available from a French firm listed in the section on sources.

That tang becomes welcome and appetizing, though, when sorrel is mixed with other greens in a salad or casserole, or cooked in soup. Try both the cream soup, using one-third to one-half cup of chopped young sorrel leaves to two quarts of milk, or the French version using sorrel cooked for five minutes in good rich chicken broth in about the same proportion. For a final touch, whip five egg yolks

with a wire whisk. Mix a cup of the hot broth into the whipped yolks in two additions, a half cup at a time. Then stir the egg-broth mixture slowly into the hot soup, which you've removed from the heat. Serve immediately. I suppose the purist would shudder, but we like chopped, braised onion in all our soups, and the French sorrel classics are no exception. A hint of garlic goes well with sorrel too.

SOYBEANS

Glycine max

As vegetable proteins go, that of the soybean is the most complete: soybeans are delicious, preparation is simple, and raising them couldn't be easier.

Soybeans may be grown in any area where three months between frosts is not too much to expect. Gardeners even in short-season areas often find it possible to harvest a crop by planting one of the earlier-yielding varieties. The young emerging seedling is very frost-tender, as is the mature foliage, but the beans in their pods are well protected at the end of the season by a fuzzy, well-insulated pod.

The soys we grow are one of several varieties grown especially for table food; they are lower in oil than the field soybean and superior in flavor. We save our own seed, but many seed houses carry at least one kind of edible soybean.

We like them best when they're green. At this stage, they look like small lima beans, but they have a starch-free, nutty flavor that we find even more appealing. The beans are tightly encased in a fuzzy two- to three-inch pod. Getting at them seems hopeless until you steam them for five minutes in a covered pan. (Don't steam them any longer than eight minutes, or the membrane lining the pod will get in your way.) It is a simple matter then to pop the beans out of the pods—a good excuse in September to sit on the porch for a view of the woods and the first signs of the coming fall.

After the initial steaming, we cook the soybeans in water for a half hour, then serve them buttered with new sweet potatoes, in a cheese sauce, or combined with sugar peas and bean sprouts to make an Oriental dinner. A handful of the beans added to any casserole or soup increases the staying power of the meal.

To freeze the beans, just cool and package them after popping them from the pods. I like to put both small and large packages in the

freezer so that I have some for full meals and some for supplementing other dishes.

Soybeans are grown like any other bean, except that they are slightly more frost-tender and even more tempting, if that is possible, to rabbits and deer. If you plant the seed when oak leaves are at the mouse-ear stage, you will be in tune with the plant's needs for your locality. Space the seed about an inch apart in rows three feet apart, thinning to a stand of plants spaced three to four inches apart. A sprinkling of blood meal (keep a shaker can handy) will help to deter wild visitors, but it must be repeated if rained into the soil.

Soybeans seem to be highly resistant to disease and insect damage. We have never had diseased plants. Mexican bean beetles occasionally wander over to the patch, but they don't seem to find much to do there. Japanese beetles may be more numerous, but even these have never done serious damage to our plantings. It is worthwhile to inoculate soybeans, just as you do with beans and peas. The benefits—better yield and improved soil—are the same, but you must use a special soybean inoculant containing the particular strain of bacteria that lives and works on soybean roots.

Harvest the beans in September when they begin to swell the pod. Usually we have about ten days of good green soybean picking in September. When the beans start to turn yellow, they will be less tender but still good to eat. Soon after that, though, they will dry and then shatter. The dry beans may be saved for soup, sprouting and baking . . . and to plant next year's soybean patch.

SPINACH

Tetragonia expansa—New Zealand Spinach
Basella alba—Malabar Spinach
Amaranthus gangeticus—Tampala

The usual garden varieties of spinach planted by winter-weary people are good while they last, but they don't last long. Such kinds as Bloomsdale, America and Viking bear good tender spring leaves, but it always seems to us that they've just gotten off the ground when they start to form a seed-stalk and give up. The eagerness of spinach to bolt to seed is supposedly due to its preference for cold weather; there is also some evidence that longer days in late spring trigger seed formation. Whatever the cause, we seldom get more than one picking from our early spinach planting—and even that seems to be ready at about the same time as the tender new wild perennial greens, like dock and dandelion, that we habitually gather.

While I wouldn't dream of discouraging you from planting spring spinach, I'd like to suggest that there are forms of spinach (technically belonging to other botanical groups but commonly called spinach) that you can harvest all season long, all through the long, hot days of summer.

Perhaps a sowing of one of the following long-standing (and slower-

81

starting) kinds of spinach will let you more fully enjoy the early spinach crop for what it is: a fleeting, long-awaited taste of spring green. All spinach is rich in Vitamins A and C and iron.

New Zealand spinach forms a sprawling two-foot-high plant that produces tender new leaf-shoots all summer long. Pluck the three- to four-inch tips of the shoots, taking only the young leaves. New shoots will form from the leaf axils.

Soak the seed for a day before planting to hasten germination, and

plant it out early, as soon as the soil is workable. Although it thrives in warm weather, it germinates best in cool weather. Space the plants about fifteen inches apart in rows three feet apart. In the deep South, the plants need some summer shade in order to keep producing. They're ready for use about ten weeks from planting.

Tampala may be picked within six to eight weeks after planting. It produces tender new leaves all summer—good either raw or cooked. Plant it when the ground is warm and frost unlikely—about when late iris blooms. Thin the plants to stand eighteen inches apart.

Malabar spinach is an attractive vine bearing thick, glossy, nutritious leaves all summer. The smooth leaves don't harbor sand and grit as curled, low-growing spinach leaves do. They also have less oxalic acid and consequently a milder flavor.

Plant Malabar spinach like Tampala but give it some support for

82

climbing. For an earlier crop, start plants in peat pots indoors about eight weeks before the date you expect to plant them out. Cuttings of the vine may be brought indoors to winter over. They make handsome house plants and furnish new cuttings that can be rooted to plant out the following spring.

SQUASH

Curcurbita maxima—autumn and winter squashes
C. moschata—crook-necked squashes

One of the most delightful signs of garden abundance is a heap of multi-shaped winter squash on the porch . . . warty blue Hubbard, deep green Acorn, creamy tan, thick-necked Butternut, green chunky Buttercup. It used to be that you needed a lot of room to grow these rampant ramblers, but newly developed bush types like Acorn Table King and Emerald Buttercup make it possible to grow squash in three-foot rows just like zucchini.

If you do have the room for vining winter squash and want the very best in flavor and flesh texture, choose Buttercup, with Butternut coming in as a mighty close second choice.

Winter squash are expected to keep well, protected as they are by a hard rind. Our expectations of summer squash are quite different . . . tender skin, delicate flesh, undeveloped seeds. You can't buy squash like that. Only the home gardener can be wanton enough to pick zucchini at three inches long, or patty pan squash when they reach the size of a silver dollar. That's when they're at their best. Try fingerling zucchini broiled with butter and topped with Parmesan cheese . . . or tiny patty pan rounds braised with onions and peppers.

Spaghetti squash is another delicacy that we must grow ourselves if we are to have any at all. The squash grows on a vigorous, spreading vine, producing a mature fruit about eight inches long and four inches in diameter. The flesh separates into spaghetti-like strands when the squash is cooked. To serve spaghetti squash, cook the fruit in boiling water for thirty to fifty minutes, then cut it open and fork out the meat into thin strands.

Spaghetti squash may sound like just another catalogue novelty,

83

and some will no doubt want to grow it mainly for fun and amazement. Others may agree with friends of ours who take seriously the recent medical findings implicating refined carbohydrates in the formation of blood-cholesterol problems. Growing spaghetti squash bypasses the whole rigamarole of refining, processing and packaging flour into pasta dough. Plant the seed, take care of it, and you've got something on which to ladle your spaghetti sauce. Besides, it's good!

Since squash is frost-tender, we wait until settled weather to plant the seeds—about the time of iris bloom. If the soil temperature is at least sixty-five degrees there will be little or no rotting of seed. Bush squash needs four square feet of garden space; a hill (two to three plants) of vining squash covers an area about eight to ten feet square. A shovelful of well-rotted manure in each hill gives the plant extra vigor.

If an otherwise healthy squash vine goes into an overnight decline, it's quite likely that a squash borer has destroyed a vital part of the stem. There's not much you can do once this has happened, but you can save the remaining plants by tossing some earth over a few of the vine nodes to encourage formation of auxiliary roots that can take over when and if the borer decimates part of the plant.

Burn affected vines as soon as they wither, to protect next year's crop.

Then there are squash bugs—those ugly grey groupies that gradually wear down the plants they live on by piercing the tissue and sucking the sap. We get out there in June and pick off the eggs (clusters of shiny tan or brown "poppy seeds") from the underside of the leaves. Hand pick and squash the bugs too, or trap them under boards and then destroy them. There'll always be squash bugs around—at least there are here in our garden—but if you get after them early you can have some squash for yourself, too. A regular program of hand-picking, crop rotation, burning spent vines and occasional dusting with rotenone, followed for several years, has resulted in a gradual but significant decline in insect damage to our squash and pumpkins.

SWISS CHARD

Beta vulgaris cicla

Hardy, nutritious, high yielding, easy to grow, chard will provide a season-long supply of good green leaves, using only a small amount of garden space. Given a little protection, it will often survive the winter to grow again the following spring. Because of its deep root, it is a good plant to grow in that part of your garden where a hard, compacted layer of soil (hardpan) may have developed just under the upper eight to twelve inches of topsoil. This is common in old gardens that have been plowed every year to the same depth, and also in new homes where heavy construction equipment has pressed down the soil. The deep root of chard will help to break up the hardpan and when the roots ultimately decay, they will aerate and enrich the lower layers of soil.

Since the succulent stalks deteriorate rapidly when shipped and handled, the only way to get good Swiss Chard is to raise your own. Nothing could be easier. The plant is quite generally immune to both insect and disease problems and it thrives on ordinary soil. The leaves harbor less grit and sand than those of spinach, since they are held well above the ground.

Chard seed may be planted well before the last frost, but it shouldn't be the very first crop you put in the ground. Let the soil warm up a bit first. Early maple bloom is a safe time. Choose a spot near long-season crops like parsnips and New Zealand spinach: a block of

85

vegetables close together will be easier to protect with mulch in the fall.

Space rows of Swiss chard eighteen inches apart and sow the seeds about four inches apart in the row. You will want the mature plants to stand about ten to twelve inches apart, but don't thin to that spacing from the very beginning: if you thin them gradually as they grow, you'll be able to have your crop and eat it too. The thinnings make a good addition to the soup pot. First pluck every other six-inch-tall plant. When the remaining plants start to crowd each other, thin them to six inches apart. Make the third and final thinning when the plants fill in the six-inch spacing.

Expect to harvest your chard from June until heavy frost, except in the deep South where leaf size may dwindle in summer heat. In this case, a second planting made in late May or early June will take over in midsummer.

The best-flavored leaves are those six to ten inches long. Larger leaves develop an earthy taste, so feed them to the chickens, rabbits, or the compost pile. If you keep the large outer leaves picked, you will always have a supply of new young leaves to pick for meals: a summer's worth of steamed and buttered chard, creamed chard, chard in soups and salads. The chopped and cooked stems may be prepared and served with the tops or separately, perhaps braised with onions or baked in your favorite sauce. If your family is slow to accept a large mound of greens unadorned, win them over with the following dish we've worked out in our kitchen—kind of a hybrid enchilada-blintz:

FILLING: $\frac{1}{2}$ pound ground beef

$\frac{1}{4}$ pound bulk sausage

1 onion

3 cloves garlic

1-1$\frac{1}{2}$ cups cooked, chopped chard and/or other greens

(If you prefer not to eat meat, substitute 1$\frac{1}{2}$ cups of cooked toasted buckwheat grains (kasha) and two eggs for the meat.)

Brown meat with onions; stir in chard and garlic.

Salt to taste.

BATTER: 3 eggs

1 cup milk

$\frac{1}{2}$ cup cornmeal

$\frac{1}{2}$ cup whole-grain flour

Stir eggs and milk into cornmeal-flour mixture. Spread $\frac{1}{4}$ cup of the batter thinly in a hot, oiled frying pan. Brown on one side. Do not turn. Remove pancake and spoon filling onto the center of it, then roll the thin dough around the filling. Arrange the filled rolls in a shallow oven-proof pan. Bake at 350 degrees for 30 minutes, topping with slices of sharp natural (not processed) cheese for the last 10 minutes. Serve with fresh tomatoes and minced hot peppers.

87

TOMATOES

Lycopersicum esculentum

We started growing low-acid orange tomatoes as a sideline to our main crop of regular red tomatoes. As it turned out, we like them better than some of the reds, so they now get equal billing on our garden plan. I don't know where we'd ever buy any, but each summer we have plenty of homegrown orange tomatoes to serve to guests, eat at almost every meal ourselves, and send home with friends who like their mildness and meatiness. There are several good varieties of low-acid orange or yellow tomatoes. We favor Jubilee, a round, meaty tomato of superb quality. It is exceptionally solid, with a pleasing globe shape and a luscious deep orange color. Sunray is reported to be even better, but we haven't tried it yet.

We set out our started tomato plants in mid-May, when the barn swallows have returned and all danger of frost is over. Our rows are three to four feet apart with the plants spaced two feet apart in the row. When putting tomato seedlings in the ground, I always bury the lower sets of leaves, leaving a short plant less likely to be whipped about

by wind and easier to protect if a late frost threatens. Each of those underground leaf nodes will form roots, thereby strengthening the plant. Place a strong young twig right next to the tomato stem, with half the twig above soil level and half below.

When you set out your plants, you have the choice of doing the job right (staking and consequent pruning and tying) or doing as we now do (letting them sprawl on a deep hay mulch), or trying something new (setting cylinders of wire fencing over the plants to support them as they grow). It's not that we don't *believe* in staking tomatoes —it's just that we don't have the time. We do lose some that rot on the ground, but we always seem to have plenty to eat and put away for the winter.

Plum tomatoes, also known as Italian or pear or paste tomatoes, are solid, meaty, small tomatoes of plum or pear shape, growing on vigorous spreading vines. They seem to thrive almost anywhere and, in fact, often volunteer the following season. Despite their solidity, tough skin and charming shapes, I have never seen them sold in stores. A puzzle, when they are so good. Our neighbor likes to carry them in his lunch, since they are less juicy than other kinds and easier to bite into.

We grow the plum tomatoes to free ourselves from reliance on store-bought mixes and ready-made sauces. The beginnings of a year's good eating in the form of eggplant Parmesan, barbecued pork, catsup, pizza sauce, chili sauce, baked beans, tomato chutney and the like are right out there in that patch of San Marzano or Roma—whatever variety we've put in this year. The relative dryness of this tomato's flesh requires less fuel to reduce it to a paste or sauce: nature has already concentrated it.

If you are selecting for flavor, other good tomato varieties for slicing and regular table use are Supersonic, Moreton, Big Boy and Rutgers. Manalucie is both tasty and disease resistant, good for southern gardens. Caro-Red is small but high in Vitamin A. Double-rich is—what else—doubly rich in Vitamins A and C. Oxheart is beautiful, solid and meaty with few seed cavities, if you don't mind its lateness and relatively low productivity. Good small lunchbox and snack tomatoes are Tiny Tim and the larger Red Cherry.

Flea beetles—very active, pinhead-sized insects—sometimes eat holes in leaves of young tomato plants early in the season. To control the beetles, dust the affected plants with diatomaceous earth (available as Perma-guard), a natural mineral product that destroys the insects by dehydration. Another common tomato problem is blossom-end rot, which appears as a bruised, leathery spot on the bottom of the fruit (opposite the stem end). It is caused by fluctuations in moisture and is especially likely to show up after a long drought. Hard cores in tomatoes are also caused by uneven water supply. Mulching helps to keep the soil more evenly moist.

The tomato hornworm—a light green caterpillar the size of your little finger (well, of mine, anyway!)—looks ferocious, but hesitate a moment before you destroy it. When we see the hornworm in our garden, it is almost always preyed upon by white larvae of the Ichneumon fly. They look like grains of rice adhering to the hornworm's back. Happy to see this example of natural control in our own patch, we leave them alone and go our way humming. Hornworms that are not host to these larvae should, of course, be destroyed.

WATERCRESS
Nasturtium officinale

There's something about this peppery member of the mustard family that can send otherwise sedate people mucking through cow pastures and wading in brooks to pick a handful of the fresh green leaves. The flavor of watercress is pungent, but with an elusive, pleasing overtone that is hard to describe. A good source of Vitamins A and C, it is prized as an ingredient in soup, a garnish and a sandwich filling. Cut into salads, it adds character and food value.

Watercress is a perennial that thrives on the humus-rich banks of streams of cool water, especially limestone streams. It flourishes best in running water and at least partial sun. The interlaced roots of watercress extend into the water of the stream and trap water-borne leaves which ultimately become the leaf mold that nourishes the plant.

If you have running water on your place—even a tiny stream—you can cultivate your own watercress. Even if, like most gardeners, you have no stream of your own, you may have access to a nearby stream where a few starts of watercress could flourish. Or, perhaps you'd like to try your luck at growing watercress to maturity in pots kept in trays of water, without transplanting them to a stream bed. It has been done, though not by me.

Give yourself and the plant the best possible chance. Sow the seeds in soil that approximates as closely as possible the preferred natural conditions of watercress: well-limed soil rich in leaf mold, kept constantly moist.

To start watercress plants, we scattered seed thinly in clay flower-pots. Seed may also be sown directly on the bank of the stream. Shallow bulb pots are good since they have a large surface area. We covered the pots and kept them in trays of water all the time, both while the seed was germinating and while the seedlings were growing. It's a good idea to change the water as often as you can; aim for a daily change, anyway. My guess is that the large amount of oxygen in constantly moving water may be a requirement of the plant. Stale water has little oxygen.

Be sure that the soil around the growing seedlings is moist at all times. Keep the pots with seedlings and transplants partly submerged —an inch or so—in water. Give them full sun either on a windowsill or under lights.

When the young plant is three to four inches tall and has a good root system, plant it out in the bank of the stream just above the water level. Avoid setting new plants at the outer curve of a sharp bend in the stream where heavy rains may cause a washout. Make little pockets with rocks or logs to give the plants a chance to get established and shield them from the force of the water.

Watercress will grow a foot high in a good year. You can root cuttings from well-established plants to enlarge your cress bed. The spindly, tentative-looking watercress seedlings that we planted at the edge of our pond, at the point where a small spring enters, formed a bushel-basket-sized clump of the leafy delicacy in just one season.

**but
you can
grow**

WHAT GOES ON
IN THE SOIL

This book is intended more as a guide to the growing of special quality vegetables than as a general resource on all aspects of gardening. It seems unfair, though, to say "See what you can grow!" without giving you some information about gardening techniques that can help you raise a better garden. The following chapters serve as a kind of vegetable gardeners' handbook, offering suggestions on the whole process of gardening. They should provide you with what seemed to me the most important background for raising good vegetables. From that base you should be fairly well equipped to launch your own garden, whatever you choose to grow, and to delve further into more detailed reading.

Vegetables grow from the ground up. Light, air and water are ingredients vital to growth, but the necessary medium of exchange is the soil, the "placenta of life" mentioned by Peter Farb in his book *The Living Earth*. Staggering numbers of microorganisms, most of them beneficial, live in each square inch of soil. They break the organic matter in the soil into forms usable by plants. These organisms—bacteria, molds and fungi—actually live *between* the particles of soil. Plant roots, continuously sending out new root hairs, weave between soil particles to establish their territory.

If soil is heavy, hard clay, impervious and compacted, the air between particles is squeezed out and there are no tiny spaces to support the life of helpful soil microorganisms and no room for growing roots, which need air in order to thrive.

Extremely sandy soil, on the other hand, drains so fast that there is likely to be a shortage of moisture for plant roots and microorganisms, as well as rapid leaching out of plant nutrients whenever rain falls.

95

The remedy for either of these extremes (or for the middle-ground problem soil in which you and I may be raising vegetables) is to incorporate in the soil as much organic matter as possible. Organic matter may be defined as anything that once lived: leaves, hay, straw, feathers, coffee grounds, wood chips, stable bedding.

In decaying, organic matter forms humus, a spongy, friable substance that improves the physical structure of the soil; it will aerate clay-like soil and improve the moisture-holding ability of sandy soil. Roots growing in soil with a good content of organic matter (2 percent or more) need only one-quarter the rainfall required by plants growing in poor soil (0.5 percent organic matter).

Humus helps to support the vital microbial life in the soil too, and in so doing makes available to plants a wide range of natural defenses against disease and soil predators. For example, root scabies, a fungus disease, can often be controlled by plowing under a cover crop of rye. Studies at the University of Maryland, reported by Charles Morrow Wilson in his book *Roots: Miracles Below*, showed that chopped straw incorporated into the soil seemed to encourage pseudomonas bacteria; pseudomonas lives near plant roots and produces an antibiotic lethal to many harmful fungi. In other studies, Wilson reports, soil researchers have found that large applications of high-nitrogen commercial fertilizers suppressed growth of the helpful pseudomonas.

Building up your soil's content of organic matter is probably the single most important thing you can do for your garden. Adding a variety of humus-building substances and mixing them well into the soil helps to insure your plants a good supply of trace elements— elements still little understood but known to be vital.

In addition to the carbon, hydrogen, and oxygen derived from air, water and photosynthesis (courtesy of sunlight), vegetables require, as all plants do, the major elements nitrogen, potassium and phosphorus. Stated in the simplest terms, which in no way do justice to the complexity of their functions, nitrogen specializes in leaf formation, phosphorus in root and seed growth, and potassium in the metabolism of carbohydrates and plant oils, stalk strength and plant vigor. These are the three elements in commercial chemical fertilizers.

In addition to these basic three, though, plants need lesser amounts of copper, manganese and magnesium. The trace elements—sulphur, iron, zinc, calcium, boron, and molybdenum—are required in still smaller amounts. Deficiency in any one element will shut down all processes requiring that element.

The availability of trace minerals and the optimum physiological function of the plant depend on the soil's pH, a measure of hydrogen ion activity (acidity or alkalinity) expressed as a scale running from zero to fourteen. A pH of seven is neutral; below seven is acid; above seven is alkaline. The numbers run in geometrical progression, based on a factor of ten; a pH of four indicates acidity ten times that of five, 100 times that of six, 1,000 times that of seven, and so on.

Peppers and potatoes thrive in acid soil with a pH of six or slightly under. Most other vegetables need a less acid soil with a pH from 6.3 or 6.5 to 6.8 or seven. Soil testing, using either a kit, state agricultural service or commercial soil-testing labs, can determine the pH of your soil. Most Eastern soils are on the acid side. Limestone areas run closer to neutral. Some Western soils are alkaline.

Acidity may be corrected by adding ground limestone or wood ashes to the soil. Addition of organic matter to the soil helps create a buffer to correct both excess acidity and alkalinity.

The creation of a pH-balanced, nutritive soil is the impetus behind our own method of soil improvement, outlined in the following chapter. We can recommend this method: with it, we are gradually seeing a patch of heavy clay soil become a friable, humus-rich, productive piece of ground. The natural soil-improvers we use are bulky and slow-acting, but as they decay over a period of months, they keep alive in the soil the humming microbial life that feeds and defends our plants while we're not looking.

We start even before planting with a thick layer of manure-rich animal bedding, plowed under to mix well with the soil. If possible, we spread and plow under another layer in the fall.

Powdered limestone, in the form of dolomite, adds magnesium to the soil, and will help neutralize highly acid soil. It is most effective when mixed thoroughly with the soil and applied with manure. Rock phosphate and greensand, like wood ashes, provide potash and phosphorus, and are worth spreading about every three years. Greensand also improves soil structure.

Build humus by conserving and gathering every particle of once-living matter that can be returned to your soil. Dig it in, plow it under, use it for mulch, or make a pile and compost it. Turn it into good soil that will grow more and better vegetables for you. After a year or two of this kind of program, you should begin to notice a difference in both the workability of your soil and the vitality and flavor of your crops. The rewards for the effort spent in building up your soil will be easier digging, possibly less disease and insect damage—and abundant good eating!

GARDENING ARTS FOR GROWING BETTER VEGETABLES

MULCHING

A good thick mulch spread between rows will smother weeds and save you hours of weeding time. Mulch also helps retain soil moisture and adds humus to the soil as it decays. A layer of mulch encourages earthworms; they thrive in the damp, easily-penetrated upper layers of the soil and leave their rich castings near the roots of plants. Mulch cushions developing fruits like cucumbers, melons and tomatoes and prevents rain-splashed mud from messing up lettuce and chard. Bare, wet soils often cake and repel water in a heavy rain, causing erosion—a sad thing to happen to a garden. A mulched garden absorbs rain and breaks the impact of eroding droplets.

When should you mulch?

Vegetables that thrive in cool weather—peas, potatoes, cabbage, lettuce and such—may be mulched early in the spring so that the soil will stay within the cool range they prefer for an extra week or two. We try to mulch these crops as soon as the plants show a definite row and we have a chance to round up the mulch and get it to the garden.

For crops like peppers, squash, tomatoes and cucumbers that need warm soil to thrive, wait for the ever-stronger sun to bake the soil warm. We mulch these heat-loving plants in June, when they are well established but before they begin to spread.

Some successful gardeners keep a year-round blanket of mulch on their gardens, raking it aside in the spring for the soil to warm and dry sufficiently for planting. All our crops are mulched all summer, some all winter too. About three-quarters of the summer mulch has decayed into the ground by Fall, helping maintain a good soil.

How much mulch do you need? It depends on what you are using: two to three inches of sawdust, three to four inches of shredded leaves, a five- to seven-inch "book" of baled hay, eight to ten inches of loose hay or straw, and at least that much of whole leaves. Leaves are especially mineral-rich because tree roots delve deeply into the soil to bring up minerals that would be far beyond the reaches of our digging forks. Although they break down readily, there is some evidence that when leaves are composted, their essential minerals are made even more available to growing plants than when they are simply spread on the soil.

The coarser the mulch, the more thickly it must be applied to exclude light and air from those ambitious weeds. You can mulch right over started weeds a foot or shorter if you use a heavy enough mulch.

What makes a good mulch? The mulches we like best to use are those that will improve the soil as they decompose . . . hay, leaves, grass clippings, sawdust, straw, corn cobs, wood chips, pine needles, seaweed and lake weed. Sawdust and wood chips are high in carbon and low in nitrogen, and if used fresh (not aged) should be sidedressed with blood meal or some other handy source of nitrogen, so that they don't rob the growing plants of the soil's nitrogen.

Discarded carpet strips and sheets of newspaper may be used as mulch between rows, especially if covered with a thin layer of organic material to hold them down and make the arrangement more attractive. Plastic effectively discourages weeds but adds nothing to the soil. Black plastic is sometimes worth using to warm the ground around heat-loving plants like melons and eggplant.

COMPOSTING

Making compost involves the recycling of natural materials into a once-more usable form. Into the pile go leaves, eggshells, fabric scraps,

99

vacuum sweepings, pulled weeds. Most of us have plenty of those kinds of things. Refuse. Junk. A problem. But when you start composting, you realize that this housekeeping residue has value as the start of a rich, easy-to-use plant food.

Compost will not burn plants the way commercial chemical fertilizers can. When you use it to nourish your plants, you needn't worry about those all-powerful numbers. (Now let's see, shall I get 5-10-5 or 10-12-12?) Compost, since it includes a little of this and a little of that, tends to arrive at a balanced proportion of the three major elements, at the same time including plenty of trace elements. For especially heavy-feeding plants like cucumbers, melons and such, we dig extra manure or compost into the hill, or put compost into the hole when setting the plant into the garden.

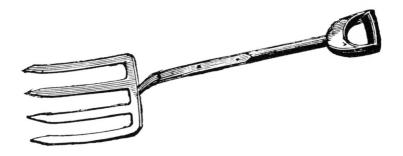

The range of ingredients that make good compost is practically unlimited. We use any unsprayed plant that is not diseased, any manures or other sources of nitrogen we might have, and whatever else happens to be available—hair clippings, expired goldfish, wood ashes, rock phosphate, weeds, old wallpaper and plaster, nut shells, feathers, grass clippings, potato peelings, seashell chips, any non-greasy garbage. *Any* manure—pigeon, rabbit, goat, hen, horse, pig, cow, llama, lion—is a valuable ingredient of the heap. Horse, sheep and chicken manure heat rapidly; cow and pig manure, having more moisture, heat more slowly.

If you don't have a rabbit hutch in your back yard or a barnful of goats, as we do, look for nitrogen-rich animal manure from zoos, steer feeding lots, university research centers, riding stables, circuses. Blood meal and fish emulsion are highly-concentrated, convenient sources of nitrogen; they lack the bulky humus-building value of manure, but nourish plants effectively. And there's always bagged dried cow manure, available at garden stores.

100

We happen to live on a farm now, but we have raised vegetables in the city and in small towns too. We feel it's pretty safe to say that the ingredients we use to improve our soil can be found in one form or another in most places. Leaves and wood chips are in fact even more likely to pile up unwanted in cities and towns than they are in the country. In addition, population centers have concentrations of industries that often produce soil-building by-products. Leather dust from shoe factories, hair clippings from barber shops and schools, coffee grounds from restaurants, sawdust from lumberyards, packing excelsior, spent hops from breweries, cannery and slaughterhouse discards are all excellent soil builders.

There are some things you *don't* want in your compost pile:

GREASY SCRAPS—The fat retards decomposition.

MEAT—It may attract unwanted animals to the pile.

DISEASED PLANTS

TOXIC SPRAYED MATERIAL

PLASTIC, ALUMINUM FOIL, STYROFOAM—any substance that will not rot.

BLACK WALNUT SHELLS—They may be toxic to some plants.

BRAZIL NUT AND COCONUT SHELLS—They are slow to decompose.

When we make compost, we like to put down a cross-hatching of old sticks and twigs to permit air circulation at the bottom of the pile. Over that we pile a good ten-inch layer of leaves, a sprinkling of other plant and food refuse, then a layer of manure up to two inches deep. The third layer is a toss of good garden soil.

And that's all there is to it: green matter (the thickest layer), a salting of manure, a sprinkling of earth. If you don't have enough ingredients at one time to layer it like this, simply toss on what you have as it becomes available. The variety will insure that you have a good pile. If you have no manure, use a sprinkling of blood meal or diluted fish emulsion to provide the nitrogen needed to start the com- posting process.

If you're using grass clippings, it's a good idea to put them in a shallow layer or mix them with other ingredients, since they do tend to mat. They also heat up rapidly, so they are well worth including in your compost.

Try to form the compost pile into a square or circle rather than a cone. To promote good heating and consequent decomposition, the pile should be three to five feet high. Higher than that is unwieldy; lower won't maintain heat. Moistening the pile helps to get it off to a good start. A few large sticks or poles poked into the pile help to admit air, on which the bacteria that break down the materials into usable compost thrive. Encourage these bacteria by turning the pile several times during the first month after you build it.

Compost can be made in as little as two weeks by shredding all the ingredients with either a rotary mower or a shredder. Materials should be well mixed and turned about three times after heating begins. More work, but fast results.

Although it isn't absolutely necessary to enclose the pile, it makes it easier to maintain proper height and shape and to keep within bounds. If your lot is small and your neighbors are close, you can still make good compost without offending anyone. Each shovelful of compost you can make will enrich your soil so that you can plant vegetables much closer together and so get more food from the same plot. A well-made compost pile has no objectionable odor and a neat, well-manicured garden won't be marred by any of the following arrangements:

A SQUARE OF PICKET FENCING or snow fencing supported by four corner stakes.

A CYLINDER OF CHICKEN WIRE set at the back of the property.

AN OIL BARREL kept in the garage—very compact, it holds an amazing amount, since things settle as they decompose.

LARGE PLASTIC BAGS—Stuff them with compost ingredients and store in odd corners.

A GARBAGE CAN with holes in the bottom and sides—it makes good compost and is acceptable in any community.

On a large lot, of course, or on a country place, you can let your pile ramble or use more makeshift means of confining it, such as concrete blocks or old boards.

A week or two after you've started your compost pile, you may notice a plume of steam rising from the center—an indication that the first stage of the cycle is proceeding on schedule. Bacterial action is turning the carbon in your heap's ingredients into heat energy. The center of the pile may heat to 160 degrees.

When the heap cools, you may want to turn it to mix the well-decayed center material with the coarse outer stuff. This keeps the decomposition process percolating along steadily.

Compost is ready to use when it has reached a black crumbly state in which the individual components have lost their identity. When still quite rough, it can be dug into garden rows. If it is in short supply, make the best use of it by putting a shovelful in the planting hole when setting out plants. There is much scientific evidence in favor of the idea that a well-nourished plant resists disease and insect attack. Experiment for yourself by dosing a problem plant with some well-made compost.

We are, all of us, slowly waking up to the fact that many things we considered disposable don't go away when we throw them out. As we survey a growing heap of terribly permanent discards, the whole process of decay and decomposition begins to assume a new respectability. There is more reason than ever, today, to make compost . . . to make use of that cycle of decay that serves us by converting a lot of apparently useless refuse into a rough but rich, unified and inoffensive form of plant food. I hope you'll try it!

GREEN MANURING

Literally homegrown soil enrichment, green manure is simply a crop grown especially for turning under rather than for harvesting. It is a neat, no-haul way to build a strong garden soil. A well-chosen green-manure planting, plowed under while still succulent, will enrich the soil, build humus, and feed valuable soil microorganisms.

You have probably noticed that good farmers plant cover crops of winter rye after harvesting corn. Even a small garden may be improved in tilth and fertility by turning under green manure crops. When a row or section of vegetables has been harvested, if you can

spare the space, broadcast seed of any of these soil-improving crops in time for it to germinate and grow a few inches before frost:

BUCKWHEAT—a quick-growing, deep-rooted plant that will give you a foothold on improving even poor soil, since it tolerates a wide range of heavy, poor and acid soil conditions. Plant it when the earth is warm.

OATS—also adaptable to a wide range of soil conditions, oats thrive in cool, moist weather.

RYE—deservedly popular as a soil-building crop because its heavy root growth contributes a lot of humus. Plant winter rye in late summer and plow it under the following spring.

WHITE CLOVER—a delicate, low-growing plant that can be planted between widely spaced garden rows to smother weeds and add nitrogen and humus to the soil when turned under.

SOYBEANS—a three-foot-tall legume which should be planted in warm weather and turned under before it sets seed. Any leguminous soil-building plant like soybeans, clover, vetch, alfalfa and field peas will grow more vigorously and leave more nitrogen in the soil if the seed is inoculated with a powder containing the correct strain of nitrogen-fixing bacteria (specific for each kind of legume and generally available from seed dealers) before planting.

Other valuable green manure crops are kale, rape, Sudan grass, field bromegrass, lespedeza, crotalaria, red and sweet clover, barley, millet and cow-horn turnip.

Any plant grown for soil enrichment should be turned under while still green and juicy, before it starts to form seed and toughen, so that it will decompose faster in the soil.

Green manuring grows plant food right in the garden, at root level, eliminating a lot of hauling and spreading of heavy, costly bags of trucked-in stuff. All you need is the seed, a well-prepared seedbed and a digging fork or rototiller. Every spear of green, buried while still on the grow, will improve your soil for the next crop.

WATERING

This aspect of growing garden vegetables is indeed an art, in our opinion, because it must be done right, and at the right time, to be effective. We seldom water our plants, but when we do, after two rainless weeks in August, for example, we water deeply so that the soil is wet at least five to six inches down. Shallow watering encourages plant roots to remain near the soil surface where they are vulnerable to drying, especially on unmulched ground. We favor either a soil soaker or a slowly trickling hose tucked under the mulch and rotated through the patch; a sprinkler loses much of its water to evaporation before it reaches plant roots.

We never water spring planted seeds; there is plenty of moisture in the soil then to encourage seed germination. When we plant seeds in hot, dry summer weather, we water the furrow first, then scatter the seed and pull dry soil over the seed, so that the soil won't bake and crust over the tender emerging shoots.

MANURE TEA

Dosing with manure tea is a time-honored and very effective method of giving a special boost to plants like cabbage and lettuce that grow well in rich soil. The recipe: fill a bucket, barrel or covered can two-thirds full of water. Drop in a burlap bag of manure or several shovelsful of manure—enough to fill the container almost to the top. Let this brew steep for a day and dip off the concentrated brown "tea," diluting it with an equal amount of water. Pour the solution around your plants at the rate of one gallon per plant.

We try to give our leafy plants a good three doses of manure tea during the season. Keep it away from the root vegetables, though; they don't need all that nitrogen.

MORE VEGETABLES FROM THE TIME YOU HAVE

Whether or not you have only limited planting space, you can get more vegetables from your plot by stretching the growing season. You may work a little harder, but the rewards—bountiful home-grown vegetables for now and for storage—are worth it, especially for the gardener with little space.

GETTING A JUMP ON THE SEASON

The single most important part of stretching the season involves starting early. If you raise seedlings indoors under lights and in cold frames, you'll have healthy plants ready to take off and grow as soon

105

as outdoor conditions are right. Your first crop will yield earlier, and provide you with space for successive early-maturing crops all through the summer and into the fall.

Starting early in this manner has another advantage. Since most of the especially desirable varieties of vegetables are available only as seed, you can combine your jump on the season with some adventure and experimentation with special vegetables like peppers, tomatoes, head lettuce, leeks and early cabbage. Vendors who sell started plants in the spring seldom offer many varieties; with a little planning you can bypass them on your way to a custom-made, high-yield garden!

Knowing your plants from the beginning can be very satisfying. You've already chosen the kind of vegetable you want—one with superb flavor, good vitamin content, perhaps special disease resistance. Now you'll have the chance to give your growing plants the best possible conditions and to select from those that germinate the strongest, most promising seedlings for planting out in the garden.

The generally accepted rule of thumb is to plant seeds indoors six to eight weeks before they may be safely planted out. If your house temperature is cool and you expect germination to be slow, you may want to stretch that to seven to nine weeks. Keeping seedlings under flourescent lights, we have found, allows us to start a bit earlier, since the plants stay stocky and green. If you are raising your seedlings on sunny windowsills, delay their start until six to seven weeks before you want to plant them out, or the plants will grow leggy and weak-stemmed from reaching for light.

Begin by preparing the growing medium in which your seeds will germinate. Some gardeners use vermiculite (heat-expanded mica rock). Others use sphagnum moss, or friable garden soil dug in the fall and kept from freezing. In her book, *Making Things Grow*, Thalassa Cruso recommends a layered starter mix for seedlings: sand on the bottom, topped by compost and then commercially bagged sterilized soil.

We start our seeds in shallow flats made of scrap wood, with sides about two inches high. On the bottom of the flat we spread a layer of torn sphagnum moss. (We gather the moss in our woods, but it is available in garden stores. When using the bagged moss, be sure to soak it in water first.) On top of the moss, we firm in a layer of good garden soil or bagged potting soil; on top of that we spread about one-half inch of dampened vermiculite. The seeds germinate in the light, moist vermiculite, and send roots down to the richer soil below. The moss on the bottom holds moisture, yet retains many air spaces, in which the roots find the oxygen they seek.

106

Sow your seed thinly in the flat, either broadcast or in rows. No seed should be less than one-half inch away from any other—crowded seedlings develop spindly, weak stems. Trust the seeds. They look small, but they'll come up. Give them room.

Fine seeds may be scattered and gently pressed into the damp vermiculite. Larger seeds may be covered lightly with an additional thin layer of vermiculite. If you have moistened the growing medium, you won't need to water the flats, and can avoid washing seeds out of place. If the flats do seem dry, dip your fingers into water and shake the drops off lightly onto the soil.

Mark the flats with the variety and the date sown. Then provide the conditions they need for germination:

MOISTURE—It is enough to retain the moisture already present in the flat by covering it with plastic or foil, or by setting another flat on top of it. We have tried enclosing the flats in plastic bags, but have found that the lack of air circulation encourages mold formation.

WARMTH—Seeds will germinate much more rapidly at temperatures averaging seventy to eighty degrees than they will at fifty to sixty degrees. We keep our seedling flats in a warm corner near the Franklin

stove. Expect to see emerging seedlings in one to three weeks, depending on the kind of seed and the temperature during germination.

DARKNESS—Seeds are dormant bits of life, containing within themselves everything they need to grow until the first true leaves take over. Most vegetable seeds have no need for the stimulation of light while germinating; they are programmed from within. (A few ornamentals like coleus and snapdragons do need light to germinate completely.)

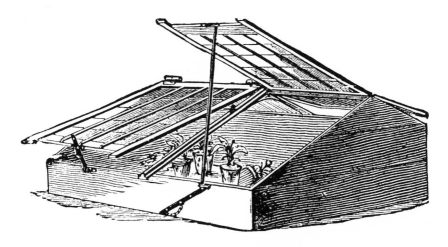

As soon as the seedling has emerged from the soil surface, though, it needs light, and the sooner the better. Seedlings kept in the dark for as long as a day develop long, pale, weak stems. So it is important to make a careful daily check of the seedling flats so that germinating seedlings may be given light.

We have raised good seedlings on sunny southern windowsills, but there are not enough windowsills for all the special vegetable plants we want to start early. We now use fluorescent lights to nurse our spring seedlings along, with wonderful results. You don't need the special growing tubes, either; a combination of one cool-white and one warm-white tube will do just as well. We keep the plants as close as possible to the tubes, just short of touching, to promote sturdy stems and green leaves. Ideally, the plants should receive around sixteen hours of light a day; ours make do with around twelve hours, in rotating round-the-clock shifts. Occasionally we'll give a flat of seedlings a full twenty-four hours of light, but never regularly; the plant needs darkness to convert products of photosynthesis into forms it can use as food.

108

Before the seedlings develop their first true leaves, they should be thinned to stand no closer than an inch apart each way. Snip off the extras with a small scissors; pulling them may tear entangled roots of the seedlings you've chosen to keep.

The first leaves you will see on your seedlings are the cotyledon or seed leaves—less differentiated, rudimentary leaves that carry the plant along until its characteristic true leaves develop. If you intend to transplant your seedlings from their flats to larger flats or individual pots, you should do so after the first true leaves have formed and before the second set of true leaves appears. We routinely transplant all but cucurbit seedlings for two reasons: we can select the best plants on the basis of good root development as well as top growth, and transplanting stimulates root growth.

We set our transplants in peat pots or in larger flats spaced two inches apart each way. Our potting soil varies from year to year according to what we have around, but we base it generally on Thalassa Cruso's recommended mixture of equal parts of soil (from garden or bagged potting soil), shredded sphagnum moss, peat moss or leaf mold, and Perlite or sharp sand. We always tuck a small damp wad of sphagnum moss at the bottom of each seedling pot or layer it at the bottom of a flat.

When lifting seedlings, hold them by the first leaves rather than the succulent, easily bruised stem. Water them as you set them in their places and shield them from strong light and dry air for a day. Try to keep them growing steadily. Probably more seedlings are killed by overwatering, which drives out air spaces and rots roots, than by drying.

Newly transplanted seedlings have no need for fertilizer; they are busy developing new feeder roots. But about two weeks after transplanting, and every two weeks thereafter until we plant them out, we give our seedlings a feeding of diluted fish emulsion. We sprout seeds of mung beans and alfalfa in jars in our kitchen for use as winter vegetables and find that water from soaking or rinsing the sprouts has a decidedly stimulating effect on seedlings.

Setting out plants at the right time, in the right way, is the mark of a seasoned gardener. It is easy to undo the work of months, overnight, by poor timing or insufficient protection. If in doubt about when to plant out, wait a week. Pay more attention to existing weather conditions than to absolute calendar dates.

The young plants need a period of adjustment to the ultraviolet light they receive outdoors. They also need protection from drying winds. Begin the hardening-off process by exposing the plants to increasing amounts of direct sunlight in a sheltered place, beginning

109

with an hour or two a day and increasing exposure over the period of a week or more.

Plants that thrive in cool weather—lettuce, cabbage, and the like—may be planted out a month before the date of the last expected frost. Frost-sensitive vegetables like tomatoes and peppers shouldn't be planted out in the open until danger of frost is past, although they may be grown in cold frames earlier. Stand ready to protect these tender plants from an untimely late frost, especially the week before a full moon, when, according to country folk wisdom, spring and fall frosts are especially likely to strike. I don't know why this should be true, but I take the adage seriously, having recorded the timing of frosts in my own garden over the last few years.

When you are ready to plant them out, be sure to firm the seedlings well into the soil, so that there are no air pockets surrounding the roots. If possible, put a handful of compost in the planting soil, where it will be much more effective than it would be as a top-dressing. Continue to protect the plants for at least part of the day (with berry baskets, cans or mulch) from drying winds and high sun.

You may want to keep an extra flat of seedlings as back-up insurance in case total disaster (escaped hens, hungry rabbits or severe weather) decimates a planting.

One of the special pleasures of gardening—second only, perhaps, to the gathering of good food—is the sight of a thriving row of hand-raised seedlings growing greener and sturdier by the day. Spring begins early when you raise your own.

STRETCHING THE SEASON

Getting an early start on things may require the most planning, but it is by no means the only way to stretch your growing season and improve yield: it lays an important groundwork for a whole system of gardening that will yield plentifully throughout the summer and into the fall.

Early-maturing crops (lettuce, peas and turnips, for instance) will give you an early harvest. Comb the seed catalogues for extra-early varieties that can move your first harvest date up a week or more. Plant plenty of these vegetables, and then, whenever a row stops producing, plant successive crops of quick-maturing vegetables in its place. Bush beans, radishes, lettuce and kohlrabi may be planted at two-week intervals throughout the summer. Special summer plantings of fall vegetables like celeriac, rooted parsley, beets, carrots, rutabagas, endive and winter radishes will give you good fall harvests. Try to

110

alternate root, leaf and seed crops in succession. Keep as much of the garden growing as much food as possible for as long as you can.

When colder weather sets in, you can take some simple measures to protect growing crops from frost. Move lettuce and endive seedlings into a cold frame, and protect your best two or three tomato plants under a storm window set on hay bales. Mound leaves around and over late beets and other root crops, and keep old blankets and bags handy for quick protection from weather. These things are all easy to do, and assure you of goods from the garden well after frost does come.

MORE VEGETABLES FROM THE SPACE YOU HAVE

A tiny garden, well planned, can produce an amazing amount of first-rate food. Even gardeners with plenty of land will find creative satisfaction in making good use of the space they have. Many space-saving techniques save time in the long run too.

If you find yourself wanting to plant more than you think you have room for, you can do a number of things to help you get more out of your garden than you ever thought possible.

RECONSIDERING THE NATURE OF THE VEGETABLE

VEGETABLES ARE BEAUTIFUL! There is no reason, other than stiff convention, why they cannot be grown in the front yard, along paths, by the mailbox or at the front door. Eggplant, for example—from the star-shaped lavender flower to the voluptuous satiny purple fruit—is too pretty to hide by the back fence. Hot peppers and cherry peppers present their bright, glossy fruits on sturdy plants that look especially handsome against dark green foundation plantings. Bush beans edging the path to the front door . . . why not? Put your herb garden in the front yard and plant a pumpkin vine by the mailbox. Edge a flower border with chives, lettuce or parsley. Look at your vegetables again with a new eye. See their decorative possibilities. And plant them wherever you want, without apology!

LET CLIMBING PLANTS CLIMB! Cucumbers will ramble their way up a fence; pole beans grow up rather than out; tall peas can climb brush or netting. Use of vertical space saves ground room and often results in cleaner, shapelier fruit. Even without digging new ground, you can significantly increase your harvest by using existing fences, tree trunks, posts, trellises—even outgrown swing sets—to support climbing vegetables. Use soft cloth strips to tie climbers to their supports. Heavy fruit like pumpkins may be supported by a cloth sling tied to a fence or a small shelf nailed to a trellis.

USE BUSH VARIETIES. Some notorious garden ramblers like squash and pumpkins have been tamed by plant breeders to bush form. If even the bush form takes too much space in the heart of your garden, consider using one such plant at each corner of the plot, where it can spread on two sides out over the lawn.

USING WHAT YOU HAVE

GROW WHAT DOES WELL FOR YOU. It isn't always apparent the first year, but after a few years of growing vegetables, you usually discover that there are some things that thrive willy-nilly in your soil and climate, others that produce steadily when well cared for, and still others (only a few, perhaps, but they should be recognized) which just don't seem to grow well on your piece of earth.

If your climate isn't hospitable to celery, eggplant, or pole limas, you'll save a lot of time and grief by concentrating on what *does* do well for you. Keep trying until you are sure you have done everything to give the vegetable what it needs, though. We were told that cabbage wouldn't do well here on our mountainside farm. We smiled about that last year as we shredded our way through ten gallons of sauerkraut. All the cabbage needed was more humus, which we supplied by plowing under more leaves and manure; and an extra nitrogen boost, which we provided in several doses of manure tea.

FILL IN GAPS IN THE ROW. Most gardens have little gaps from time to time where a plant was lost to frost, unearthed by the dog, killed by insects or stepped on by the gardener. Sometimes you don't know

113

what happened to it. Cause and effect are not always obvious in the garden. Anyway, you have a bare spot that will grow weeds if you let it. Keep it producing good food for you instead. Plant something there: a few lettuce seeds, a broccoli seedling, a late bush of zucchini. There's no reason for garden rows to end the season in complete uniformity. Our rows often begin in lettuce and end in beets, with a cauliflower or two punctuating the middle. It may look odd from the air, but we eat well!

114

USE SHADY AREAS. Light shade, either from trees or from taller plants, will actually improve your crop of lettuce in the summer. Parsley, chives, filbert bushes and raspberries often thrive in partial shade. Most other vegetables require full sun to do their best.

PLANT ODD CORNERS OF YOUR PROPERTY. That spot by the back step, an odd triangle at the end of the yard, pathways and driveway edgings—all can be perfectly productive, and in fact easy to tend since you can reach them from two sides. Why grow weeds by your garage when you can raise leeks, zucchini or beans instead?

DO YOU NEED ALL THAT LAWN? When my husband's mother came from Europe to live with us some years ago, she was bewildered when she saw the grassy back yard of our long, narrow city plot. Why hadn't we dug up the back lawn to plant vegetables? All that potential garden space wasted on grass! (Our plantings were arranged in conventional form at the back of the yard.) We were amused at the time, but we see now that we could have eaten very well indeed from that yard had we gone along with her old-world practicality.

I'm not going to suggest that you dig up the *whole* lawn. But you might want to consider turning a three- to four-foot strip of sod over to vegetables. It could support two rows of crops from April to November—that many more fresh delicacies for your table.

If you do decide to dig up sod, make things easy for yourself by piling up newspapers, old carpet, boards or other opaque materials over the grass for a month or so before digging. With the top growth thus squelched, the sod will disintegrate more readily. Since you probably won't be able to achieve a fine tilth in the new strip the first season, plant coarse seeds like peas, beans or soybeans there. They will improve the soil too.

PLANTING INTENSIVELY

PLANT VEGETABLES AS CLOSE AS POSSIBLE. A small, intensively planted garden can be far more gratifying than a large, poorly tended lot. If your space is limited, make the best of it by leaving only foot-room between rows of non-spreading vegetables. Study your garden layout to see where you could eliminate a path or two and thus add a row. Plant vegetables like lettuce, carrots, endive, beans, beets and onions in eight- to twelve-inch wide bands rather than single-file rows. Some extra care is needed in the beginning to keep the wide band thinned and weeded, but when the plants are well under way they shade out weeds and retain ground moisture.

In order to get away with planting intensively over a period of years,

115

you will need to feed your soil very well to keep organic matter, fertility and mineral content at high levels.

PRACTICE DOUBLE CROPPING. Put a row of lettuce between the rows of parsnips and salsify: it'll be grown and eaten before the root vegetables need the room. Plant bush bean seed in a row of lettuce as you thin and use the lettuce. Pumpkins can grow at the edge of the corn patch, peas next to young corn, radishes close to squash. Dovetailing the needs of different crops is creative gardening at its best.

PLANT VEGETABLES IN CONTAINERS. Cucumbers, lettuce, tomatoes, red peppers and chives are good candidates for this treatment. Patio Pick cucumbers and Red Cherry, Tom Thumb, Presto or Small Fry tomatoes do well in a confined space. The container can be a window box, large drain tile, clay pot or large can. It is important to provide for drainage: put an inch or two of coarse gravel in the bottom of the container. It is equally important not to fill the container with soil to the very top—leave enough space for a generous watering. Container-grown plants dry more quickly than those in the garden row, and since their roots are confined, need your very best soil, with plenty of humus in it, to hold moisture.

With measures like these, most of them requiring just a little imagination, you can produce enough special vegetables to change forever any conventional ideas you may have about where they belong. You can pride yourself on your ingenuity and efficiency as you gather another armload of squash, beans or bright peppers.

WHEN THE BUGS COME

Like it or not, we should recognize that the bugs were here first. It could be that in their scheme of things, we are the interlopers. Still, it is not unreasonable to expect a few vegetables for ourselves.

How can you control the damaging insects in your garden without knocking out the many helpful species? What will really get rid of them without tainting your food or water supply with long-lasting alien compounds? There is no single method of control that will safely eliminate bug problems from your garden. Perhaps it is just as well that this is so. Nothing should be that simple. There are, however, many effective non-toxic ways of keeping predacious insects within acceptable bounds. In some cases you can effectively eliminate them.

When we have more competition from insects than we can tolerate,

116

we first look carefully to assess the nature of the damage and the kind of insect responsible. Identify the culprit. Learn to tell the difference between a flea beetle, a Mexican bean beetle and a squash bug. How does the insect feed? Does it chew leaves, suck sap, or invade a main stem? When we know what's happening, we can defend our plants realistically. No sense spraying right and left against cutworm when all that's needed is a simple mechanical device—a stick—to protect each plant.

117

Then we consider the following insect control options, ones we find acceptable, and choose the angles of defense or attack that will affect the troublesome predator enough to make a difference.

DEFENSE

GARDENING METHODS that help your plants in other ways will sometimes fend off insects too. For example, mulching controls the Colorado potato beetle by impeding the progress of the potato bug from the soil, where it hatches, to the leaf, where it feeds. Similarly, hoeing around affected plants early in the season disturbs the life cycle of the leaf miner.

ROTATING CROPS prevents build-up in any one part of the garden of an entrenched population of specific vegetable foes. Rotation is especially important, we think, in the case of radish maggots, bean beetles and squash bugs.

COMPANION PLANTING pairs a strong guardian plant, often aromatic, with a vulnerable crop that needs protection. One of our most successful companion plantings has been the use of rings of radishes planted around hills of cucurbits (squashes, pumpkins, cucumbers) to repel the disease-carrying striped cucumber beetle. Planting pungent-smelling marigolds at intervals in the garden cuts down the nematode population; the marigolds produce a root exudate that nematodes find irritating. Many more protective combinations have been verified by experienced gardeners, among them mint to repel the cabbage moth, horseradish to ward off the potato beetle, tomatoes to keep away asparagus beetles and garlic to discourage aphids. The reason for the effectiveness of these measures is little understood, but it is all too easy to call something mere folklore or wishful thinking when we just don't understand how it works. We are only beginning to explore the subtle mechanism of root chemistry as it affects soil life and other plants. According to Charles Wilson, writing in *Roots: Miracles Below*, each species of plant has its own particular root chemistry: why leave it to the scientists to discover the implications of this basic finding? Gardeners can experiment too!

CHOOSE RESISTANT VARIETIES of vegetables, especially cucumbers, cabbage in yellows-infested areas, tomatoes where blight and bacterial wilt are problems and lettuce in mosaic-troubled areas. Select from the many catalogue offerings the vegetables bred to withstand the insect and disease problems common in your area.

TIMING CAN BE CRITICAL: forewarned is forearmed. If you know that flea beetles and aphids are especially active in your area early

118

in the season, it is sometimes worth delaying planting for a week or two so that you can set out a stronger plant. We always make a large late planting of green beans that will bear in cooler weather when bean beetles are on the wane. Observe and record your own local conditions so that you can prevent some insect damage by timing alone.

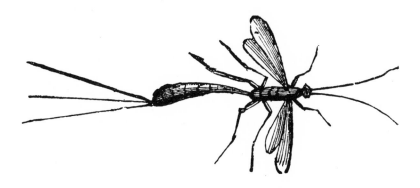

ATTACK

TRAPPING PESTS like slugs and squash bugs under boards or large leaves may not eliminate large numbers of predators, but with this method you have assured elimination of the pests you do catch, along with a certain satisfaction of knowing you've done something definite about the problem.

HAND PICKING, like trapping, may not rid your garden of every unwanted bug, but practiced regularly as you harvest your vegetables, the method can reduce significantly the number of reproducing insects in your garden. It also gives you the opportunity for righteous revenge!

BIOLOGICAL CONTROLS include the use of diseases and insect predators specific to certain unwanted insects. These methods are often very selective; usually they give a high level of control. Milky spore disease dooms Japanese beetles. Lady bugs prey on aphids and other pests. *Bacillus thuringiensis* produces disease in larvae of Lepidopterae (moths and butterflies). The tiny trichogramma wasp controls the codling moth when garden debris is cleared away and the wasp's hatching is properly timed to coincide with the egg laying

119

of the moth. Much good work has been done—and continues—in this area. What *we* wish for now is an otherwise amiable Purple-Spotted Squash Bug Eater. There must be one somewhere!

IRRITATING SUBSTANCES can discourage invading insects. Harmless tactics like putting flour or sour milk in cabbage to foul up the cabbage worm, spreading sand, ashes or glass wool to discomfit the slug, spraying hot pepper solution to drive off chewing insects—these are easy and effective remedies. A mechanical irritant of proven effectiveness is diatomaceous earth, which kills insects by puncturing their skeletal frames with microscopically sharp particles, resulting in death by dehydration.

NON-TOXIC PLANT-DERIVED INSECTICIDES like rotenone, ryania and pyrethrum are our recourse when other methods fail. We don't use them routinely, because although they are not toxic to warm-blooded creatures, they can't discriminate between the helpful insect predators (like ladybugs, lacewing flies and ground beetles), and the undesirables we want to eliminate. Rotenone *is* toxic to fish. The effectiveness of these plant toxins is short-lived, however; they readily disintegrate in a matter of days, so they are well worth using if a crop is seriously threatened.

DESTROYING AFFECTED CROPS might seem overcautious, but at the end of the season we burn seriously infested bean plants and cucurbit vines rather than composting them or feeding them to our animals. Then we're sure that any insect eggs clinging to them have been eliminated.

COOKING YOUR
HOMEGROWN VEGETABLES

Putting interesting, full-flavored, vitamin-rich vegetables on the table is a far more valid proof of cooking skill than virtuosity in baking cakes or raising soufflés, impressive as those accomplishments may be. For it is the vegetables that are most likely to be shortchanged in our supermarket gastronomy. The more processed food you eat, the greater your need for the fiber, minerals and vitamins found in the original vegetable.

When you have spent effort and time in growing the best vegetables obtainable, you will want to prepare them with respect, keeping their goodness intact. There are steps you can take to minimize loss

120

of flavor and nutrients in that basket of fresh vegetables you've picked, with much justifiable pride, from your flourishing garden. Food scientists have these things all worked out. It's just up to us to put the principles into practice.

PICKING VEGETABLES

The fresher the better. When possible, pick vegetables the last few minutes before cooking, except for salad greens which need a few hours chilling to become crisp. Vitamin content of top growth, according to Adelle Davis in *Let's Cook It Right*, is highest at the end of a sunny day.

Young vegetables are tender, cook quickly, have excellent delicate flavor. One exception in our household: green beans, which we like fairly mature, though not tough, for fullest flavor.

PREPARING VEGETABLES

Any vegetables picked ahead of time should be quickly chilled. Chilling vegetables before cutting them minimizes vitamin loss.

Never soak any vegetable in water. Vitamin C and some B vitamins are water soluble. If necessary to wash a vegetable, rinse it quickly in running water.

Scrape, don't peel, root vegetables. A high concentration of vitamins

and minerals lies just under the skin. Gouging them out is self-defeating. Whenever possible, leave vegetable skin intact while cooking.

For a gourmet salad, treat the greens well. Wash them quickly, whirl them dry in a wire basket and chill them. Then tear the leaves (don't cut them) into the salad bowl. To retain crispness, toss the leaves in oil to seal their surfaces before adding vinegar and salt. Otherwise juice is drawn out of the leaves and left in the bowl.

COOKING VEGETABLES

When boiling vegetables, have the water boiling in the pot before adding the vegetables. This fills the pot with steam which drives off vitamin-destroying air. Better yet, when possible cook vegetables by steaming rather than immersing them in large amounts of water, to conserve water-soluble flavor and food value. Save all cooking water. Add it to the soup pot or use it for gravy or baking.

Sautéing vegetables in oil seals cut surfaces from oxygen and keeps in flavor and juices. If frying vegetables, avoid overheating the fat. Toxic substances form in fats at temperatures over 360 degrees.

If vegetables are to be baked, steam them first for rapid penetration of heat. Slow heating wastes vitamins. For a change, try baking beets. To bake winter squash, halve the squash, steam unpeeled until thoroughly hot and bake cut side down till tender. To serve, fill the hollow with butter, chopped nuts, honey, parsley or whatever you like.

Cook vegetables only until tender, not a minute more. Experiment by stopping short of the flabby-vegetable stage. Tender-crisp vegetables are more colorful and nutritious. Rather than continuing to cook already tender vegetables until the family assembles, start them a bit later and let the family wait. Often vegetables can complete cooking while other foods are served. Shredded vegetables cook quickly. Try shredding beats, turnips, rutabagas, celeriac, parsnips and salsify.

If you salt vegetables, wait until cooking is complete. Salt draws out vegetable juices, losing flavor and food value to the cooking water.

Never add soda to green vegetables to retain color; it destroys B vitamins. Instead, if you wish to protect color, cook the vegetable in milk at simmering temperatures until just tender. Milk protein neutralizes the compounds that cause discoloration. This same method helps "strong-flavored" vegetables like cabbage and cauliflower remain mild. The strong flavors come from the breakdown of sulfur compounds in the vegetable at high temperatures.

122

Greens are such valuable foods that you should take special measures to make them welcome on the menu. Wash the leaves quickly but thoroughly to eliminate grit. Chop them in small pieces or cut them with kitchen shears so they won't be stringy. Avoid overcooking in large amounts of water, which can cause a bitter or astringent taste. Try cooking greens in milk or cream sauce; the milk protein will neutralize sharp plant acids. We find that sautéing greens (braising, actually, since we cover the pan) retains good flavor and texture. Mix bland and pungent greens in different proportions until you arrive at a combination that pleases you.

Simple culinary tricks like these—common sense, really, once you know something about the natural goodness of fresh vegetables—can make even the plainest meal mouthwatering. You may even reform someone who thinks he or she hates vegetables; the likelihood is they've never really *tasted* vegetables!

SOURCES FOR SEEDS AND OTHER ESSENTIALS

SEEDS BY MAIL

Seeds are one of the few remaining bargains to be found anywhere. True, you must spend some time and energy to help them on their way—but where else, for the price of a single head of shipped-in lettuce, can you get as much potential value as in a packet of seeds?

Colorful seed packet racks are enticing, but they seldom offer the best obtainable varieties of vegetables. Hardware stores, especially in

small towns, often sell seed by the ounce, weighed out just for you. The range of selections is usually limited to the old standbys, but among them you'll find some good lettuce, parsnips, cabbage and beans. Generally, the varieties offered are those known to do well in the immediate area.

By far the best way to get the whole picture of what's open to you as a gardener—really only hinted at in this book—is to send for some seed catalogues and order seed by mail. The seed houses described briefly here all offer mail-order catalogues; unless otherwise noted, the catalogues are free.

1. Burgess Seed and Plant Company, P.O. Box 3000, Galesburg, Michigan 49053

Carries a good many of the special vegetables listed here. Excellent tomato selection.

2. Burnett Brothers, 92 Chambers Street, New York, New York 10007

A surprisingly varied selection of vegetables, in seven black-and-white pages at the end of thirty-eight pages of flower seeds. A few hard-to-find treasures sprinkled in.

3. Burpee Seeds, Warminster, Pennsylvania 18974; *also* Clinton, Iowa 52732 *and* Riverside, California 92501.

A standard. Reliable, complete, with many developed-by-Burpee varieties.

4. William Dam Seeds, West Flamboro, Ontario, Canada LOR 2KO.

A fine selection of choice varieties, under multi-lingual headings, and including some very unusual foods like edible burdock and globe artichoke.

124

5. DeGiorgi Company, Council Bluffs, Iowa 51501.

A good source of the unexpected, like sorrel and three kinds of kohlrabi. Good descriptions of varieties and cultural directions. Has some things you'll not find elsewhere.

6. Farmer Seed and Nursery Company, Faribault, Minnesota 55021.

Although not the most complete selection, this catalogue offers a few vegetables unavailable (to my knowledge) elsewhere.

7. Henry Field's, Shenandoah, Iowa 51602.

The catalogue is heavier on nursery stock and flowers than on vegetables, but lists a pretty good selection of many of the special vegetables discussed here.

8. Grace's Gardens, 22 Autumn Lane, Hackettstown, New Jersey 07840.

This source for seeds of rare, interesting and extra-large vegetables sometimes offers free packets of test seed to gardeners willing to grow them carefully and report their evaluation. They ask twenty-five cents for the catalogue.

9. Gurney Seed and Nursery Company, Yankton, South Dakota 57078.

You'll need the index (if you can find it!) in this big, folksy catalogue; it's not the best organized, but it is fun to read and the source of some worthwhile unusual varieties.

10. Harris Seeds, Moreton Farms, Rochester, New York 14624.

Sober, true-blue catalogue with dependable vegetable descriptions and many fine varieties. If Harris says a vegetable is good, it's worth trying.

11. Charles Hart Seed Company, 304 Main Street, Wethersfield, Connecticut 06109.

A smallish catalogue, but it hits the highlights of the best uncommon vegetables mentioned here and, like Burnett, has some nice surprises that are hard to find elsewhere. Straightforward; no purple prose.

12. J. L. Hudson, Seedsman, P. O. Box 1058, Redwood City, California 94064.

Big on flowers, but also a good source of many old, dependable vegetable varieties at low prices. Sends vegetable catalogue for a thirteen-cent stamp.

13. Johnny's Selected Seeds, Albion, Maine 04910.

Mostly open-pollinated varieties, with many special Oriental and European strains. Personal, careful, no hype. Offers a seed swap service. Catalogue sent to new customers for fifty cents, credited toward your first order.

14. J. W. Jung Seed Company, Randolph, Wisconsin 53956.

A general catalogue, specializing in northern-grown seed.

15. Earl May Seed and Nursery Company, Shenandoah, Iowa 51603.

Appetizing color photos of many of the choice varieties of vegetables.

16. The Natural Development Company, Bainbridge, Pennsylvania 17502.

A well-chosen selection of dependable seeds; many are Burpee varieties.

17. Nichols Garden Nursery,
1190 North Pacific Highway,
Albany, Oregon 97321.

Mimeo catalogue of unusual, old, dependable and imported varieties. Dotted with useful cooking and storing hints. Strong on herbs too. Catalogue is twenty-five cents.

18. Olds Seed Company,
P. O. Box 1969, Madison, Wisconsin 53701.

Good complete listing and prompt service. A fine all-around catalogue.

19. Park Seed Company,
Greenwood, South Carolina 29647.

Enticingly illustrated selection of many good vegetables at the end of a large flower catalogue. One of the few mail-order sources of Jerusalem artichokes and seed for sweet cherry peppers.

20. Rohrer Seedsmen,
Smoketown, Pennsylvania 17576.

Limited selection of vegetable seeds, but a very complete listing of soil-improving green manure crops.

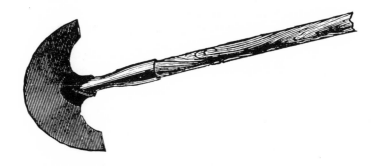

21.   Seedway, Hall, New York 14463.

Clear, well-organized listing of many good special vegetable varieties.

**22.   R. H. Shumway, Seedsman,
Rockford, Illinois 61101.**

Nostalgic turn-of-the-century illustrations, many old traditional varieties.

**23.   Stokes Seeds, Inc.,
P. O. Box 548, Buffalo, New York 14240;
and Stokes Seeds Ltd.,
St. Catherine's, Ontario, Canada L2R 6R6.**

Extensive listings in most vegetable categories, reliably described, with helpful cultural directions. A fine gardener's sourcebook.

**24.   Sutton's,
161 Bond Street, London, England.**

A British firm with an excellent reputation.

**25.   Thompson and Morgan, P. O. Box 24,
401 Kennedy Boulevard,
Somerdale, New Jersey 08083;
and c/o Canadian Garden Products Ltd.,
132 James Avenue East,
Winnipeg, Manitoba, Canada R3B ON8.**

Delightful British catalogue with many good vegetable listings, well rated for flavor and food value. Gorgeous photographs.

**26.   Otis Twilley,
Salisbury, Maryland 21801.**

Carries many good special vegetable strains, and a nice selection of heat-loving vegetables . . . tomatoes, corn, cantaloupe, watermelon.

**27. Vesey's Seeds Ltd.,
York, Prince Edward Island, Canada CDA 1PO.**

Basic and dependable; carries a fair number of the special vegetables discussed in this book.

**28. Vilmorin Seeds,
228 Quai de la Megisserie, Paris, France 75001.**

An old, respected French firm. Some of their selections are carried by a good American house, Jardin des Gourmets, Ramsay, New Jersey 07446.

**29. Vermont Bean Seed Company,
Way's Lane,
Manchester Center, Vermont 05255.**

Lots of good eating (and fine drawings too) on every page of this delightful catalogue. More peas, green and shell beans than you knew existed—world's largest selection! Soys and limas too.

TRACKING DOWN SPECIAL SEEDS

If you want to send for seed for some of the special vegetables mentioned in this book, each number following the vegetable name refers to the number assigned to a seed house in the alphabetical list above. For example, Jerusalem artichokes may be ordered from numbers 1, 2, 7, 9, 13, 15, 17 and 18 (Burgess, Burnett, Field's, Gurney, Johnny's Selected Seeds, Earl May, Nichols and Olds).

BEANS

Blue Lake   *1, 3, 4, 5, 7, 9, 10, 11, 14 through 19, 21, 23, 25, 26, 27, 29*

Contender   *2, 5, 9, 11, 15, 18, 19, 23, 26, 29*

Purple   *1, 2, 3, 6, 7, 9, 13, 16, 17, 18, 19, 22, 23, 25*

Romano   *numbers 1 through 5 (inclusive), 7, 9, 10, 15 through 18, 21, 23, 25, 26, 29*

Wade   *6, 29*

BEETS

Cylindra, also called Formanova   2 *through* 5, 7, 9, 13, 18, 19, 22, 23, 26, 27

Golden   3, 4, 7, 15, 17, 19, 23, 25

Long Season or Winter Keeper   2, 3, 5, 10, 11, 16, 23

CABBAGE

Chinese   1 *through* 23, 25, 26

Jersey Queen, also called Jersey Wakefield   2, 3, 5, 6, 7, 9 *through* 20, 22

Kraut   1 *through* 7, 9 *through* 23, 25, 26, 27

Ruby Ball   2, 3, 6, 10, 15

Savoy   1 *through* 7, 9, 10, 11, 13 *through* 19, 21, 22, 23, 25, 26, 27

CARROTS

Baby-Finger   3, 4, 21, 23, 25

Danvers Half-Long   1, 3 *through* 7, 9, 11, 12, 15, 18, 20, 22, 23, 26

Imperator   2, 4, 6, 7, 9, 11, 16, 18, 20, 23, 26

Oxheart   4, 5, 9, 22

Red-Cored Chantenay   2, 3, 4, 6, 7, 9, 11 *through* 14, 17 *through* 21, 23, 25, 27

Scarlet Nantes   1, 4 *through* 7, 10 *through* 13, 18, 19, 21, 22, 23, 25, 26

Short and Sweet, or similar carrot under other name   1, 2, 3, 6, 16, 22, 25

Tendersweet   1, 7, 9, 15, 18, 19, 22

CAULIFLOWER

Purple   *2, 3, 4, 6, 9, 10, 11, 16, 19, 22, 23*

Self-Blanche   *10, 19, 23*

CELERIAC

2, 3, 4, 5, 7, 9, 10, 12, 13, 14, 17, 22, 23, 25

CHINESE VEGETABLES

Special Assortments   *8, 13, 25*

CHIVES

1, 3 through 7, 9 through 14, 16 through 19, 21, 23, 25, 27

COMFREY PLANTS

9, 17 and from North Central Comfrey Producers, Box 195, Glidden, Wisconsin 54527

CORN

Bantam   *1 through 7, 9, 11, 12, 13, 16, 17, 18, 22, 23*

Butter and Sugar   *6, 10, 11, 21, 26*

Country Gentleman   *2, 3, 5, 9, 13, 16, 17, 18, 22*

Evergreen   *2, 3, 6, 9, 11, 12, 13, 16, 18, 20, 22*

Honey and Cream   *1, 3, 4, 9, 11, 15, 17, 21, 25*

Illini Super Sweet   *1 through 6, 9, 11, 16, 18, 19, 23, 26*

Silver Queen   *3, 4, 6, 10, 11, 15, 16, 19 through 22, 26*

Wonderful   *10*

CUCUMBERS

Burpless   *1 through 7, 9, 10, 11, 14, 15, 17, 18, 19, 21, 22, 23, 25, 26*

Gherkin   *1, 3, 4, 7, 9, 13, 15, 16, 17, 21, 22*

Lemon   *3, 4, 5, 9, 10, 12, 13, 14, 16, 17, 21, 23*

Oriental   *1, 4, 8, 10, 12, 13, 17, 23, 25*

Patio Pick   *6, 7, 15, 18, 19, 21, 23, 25, 26*

Pioneer   *11, 19, 23*

ENDIVE

2 through 7, 9, 11 through 14, 16, 18 through 23

ESCAROLE

2 through 6, 9, 11, 12, 13, 16, 18, 20 through 23, 26

FENNEL

2 through 6, 9 through 12, 16, 25

JERUSALEM ARTICHOKE ROOTS

1, 2, 7, 9, 13, 15, 17, 18

KALE

1 through 5, 7, 9 through 14, 16 through 23, 27

KOHLRABI

2 through 7, 9 through 12, 14 through 22, 25, 27

LEAF LETTUCE

Bibb   *1, 2, 3, 5, 9, 10, 11, 13, 16, 18, 20, 21, 22*

Black Seeded Simpson   *1, 3, 5, 6, 7, 9, 11, 12, 13, 15, 18, 20 through 23, 26, 27*

Buttercrunch   *1 through* 7, 9, 10, 11, *13 through* 19, 21, 22, 23, 25, 26

Matchless, also called Deer Tongue   2, 3, 5, 11, 17, 18

Oak Leaf   *1 through* 6, *9 through* 12, 13, *15 through* 22

Salad Bowl   3, 4, 6, 7, 9, 10, 11, *13 through* 17, 19, 20, 21, 25

Tom Thumb   2, 3, 5, 6, 7, 17, 19, 22, 25

LEEKS

1, 2, 5, 6, 7, *9 through* 14, *16 through* 19, 22, 23, 25, 27

OKRA

1, 2, 3, 5, 6, *9 through* 12, *14 through* 21, 23, 26

PARSNIPS

All America   2, 5, 7, 9, 10, 17, 22

Harris, also called White Model   10, 13, 18, 23, 27

Hollow Crown   *2 through* 5, 11, 12, 15, 16, 18, 20, 22, 23, 25

PEAS

Chinese Snow Peas   8

Dwarf Grey Sugar Peas   *1 through* 7, 9, 11, 12, *15 through* 19, 22, 29

Lincoln   4, 6, 10, 21, 23

Mammoth Melting Sugar   *1 through* 5, 9, 10, 13, 16, 18, 19, 20, 22, 29

Petit Pois   2, 25

Wando   *1 through* 7, 10, 13, 14, 15, 18, 21, 23, 26, 27, 29

133

PEPPERS

Banana   *3, 4, 5, 10, 18, 19, 22, 23, 26*

Bell Boy   *2, 3, 6, 7, 11, 15, 18, 19, 21, 23, 26*

Calwonder   *1 through 5, 7, 10, 11, 12, 15, 16, 18 through 21, 23, 26*

Different varieties of hot peppers   *1 through 5, 7 through 19, 21, 22, 23, 25*

Long Red Cayenne   *1, 2, 3, 5, 12, 16, 17, 18, 22, 23*

Numex Big Jim   *8*

Pimiento   *1, 3, 7, 15, 18, 19, 21, 22, 23*

Staddon's Select   *10, 13, 21, 23, 27*

Sweet Cherry   *1, 3, 5, 14, 18, 19*

Vinedale   *23*

POTATOES

2, 7, 9, 11, 13, 14, 15, 18, 19, 20

PUMPKINS

Bush type   *6, 9*

Funny Face Hybrid   *1, 9, 18, 21, 27*

Lady Godiva   *3, 4, 8, 9, 10, 19, 23, 25*

Triple Treat (Hull-less)   *3*

RADISHES

Black Spanish   *2 through 6, 9 through 12, 17, 18, 21, 22, 23*

China Rose   *7, 9, 12, 14, 15, 18, 23*

Good selection of other fall radishes   *13, 17*

Sakurajima   *1, 7, 8, 9, 12, 17, 22*

Short-Top Scarlet Globe   *5*

ROOTED PARSLEY

Hamburg   *3, 5, 9 through 14, 17, 18, 22, 23*

SALSIFY

2 through 6, 10, 11, 12, 15 through 18, 20 through 23, 25

SOIL-IMPROVING CROPS

9, 13, 20, 22, 25

SORREL

2, 5, 11, 12, 13, 17, 25

SOYBEANS

3 through 7, 9 through 13, 15, 16, 17, 19, 20, 21, 23, 25, 29

SPINACH

Malabar   *3, 17*

New Zealand   *2 through 7, 9, 10, 12, 14, 16, 17, 18, 21, 22, 23*

Tampala   *1, 3, 16, 19*

SQUASH

Bush Acorn   *3, 5, 6, 9, 10, 11, 13 through 16, 18, 19, 21, 22, 27*

Buttercup   *1 through 7, 9 through 15, 18, 21, 22, 23, 26, 27*

Butternut   *1 through 7, 9, 10, 13 through 16, 18, 19, 21, 26*

Eat-All   6

Spaghetti   *1, 3, 4, 5, 7, 8, 9, 13, 15, 17, 18, 19, 21, 22, 23, 25*

Sweetnut   6

SWISS CHARD

1 through 7, 9 through 23, 26, 27

TOMATOES

Caro-Red (high Vitamin A)   *1, 9, 14, 23, 25*

Doublerich   *16*

Jubilee   *3, 15 through 19, 22*

Manalucie   *1, 2, 3, 19, 26*

Moreton   *10*

Pear and Plum tomatoes   *1 through 7, 9 through 19, 21, 22, 23*

Rutgers   *2, 3, 5, 6, 7, 10, 11, 12, 16, 18, 19, 20, 22, 26*

Sunray   *1, 2, 3, 7, 8, 10, 18, 21*

Supersonic   *10*

WATERCRESS

3, 5, 10, 11, 12, 16, 22, 23

OTHER USEFUL SUPPLIES

NON-PERSISTENT, RELATIVELY SAFE INSECTICIDES

Rotenone   *2, 4, 7, 10, 19*

Rotenone, pyrethrins and ryania mixed   *16*

Diatomaceous earth   *4, 9, 19*

136

BIOLOGICAL CONTROLS

Thuricide, a preparation of BACILLUS THURINGIENSIS *3, 4, 6, 7, 9, 14, 17, 18*

Ladybugs *3, 9*

Praying mantis egg cases *3, 9*

These and other controls also available at:

Gothard, Inc., Box 370, Canutillo, Texas 79835

Eastern Biological Control Company, Route 5, Box 379, Jackson, New Jersey 08527

LIQUID SEAWEED EXTRACT

6, 10, 18, 22, 23, 29

Also available at: Zook and Ranck, Gap, Pennsylvania 17527

SOYBEAN INOCULANT

18, 22, 29

INOCULANT FOR GARDEN PEAS AND BEANS

Available from most seed companies.

FISH EMULSION CONCENTRATE

2, 4, 7, 9, 14, 16, 17, 18

COMPOST BIN KIT

6, 7, 9, 14, 18, 22, 25

FLUORESCENT LIGHT TUBES AND FIXTURES

3, 7, 13, 14, 18, 20

Also available through household mail-order catalogues like Sears, Penney's, Wards.

PARMESAN CHEESE

Mentioned several times in the vegetable chapters, Parmesan is a richly flavored cheese that combines well with many vegetable dishes. It is also, according to Frances Moore Lappe, writing in *Diet for a Small Planet,* the highest in protein of any cheese.

If all that's available to you is the cardboard shaker-tube of Parmesan found on supermarket shelves, I'll let you in on our source of supply for a really first-rate Parmesan, sold by the hunk (or the wheel, for that matter): Eau Galle Cheese Factory, Eau Galle, Wisconsin 54737. The cheese factory is a small white building in a little Wisconsin hamlet. The last I heard, the Parmesan was made right there. Wisconsin is dotted with cheese factories and I'm sure there are other good sources of Parmesan cheese; this happens to be the one we know and have dealt with, both in person and by mail.

SOME HELPFUL BOOKS

GENERAL GARDENING ADVICE

CARLETON, R. MILTON. *Vegetables for Today's Gardens.* Princeton, New Jersey: D. Van Nostrand, 1967.

CRUSO, THALASSA. *Making Things Grow Outdoors.* New York: Alfred A. Knopf, 1976.

FARB, PETER. *Living Earth.* New York: Harper & Row, 1959.

ORTLOFF, H. STUART, and RAYMORE, HENRY B. *A Book About Soils for the Home Gardener.* New York: William J. Morrow, 1972.

STOUT, RUTH. *How to Have a Green Thumb Without an Aching Back.* New York: Cornerstone Library, 1974.

WILSON, CHARLES MORROW. *Roots: Miracles Below.* Garden City, New York: Doubleday, 1968.

MULCH

CAMPBELL, STU. *The Mulch Book: A Guide for the Family Food Gardener.* Charlotte, Vermont: Garden Way Publishers, 1974.

COMPOST

CAMPBELL, STU. *Let It Rot! The Gardener's Guide to Composting.* Charlotte, Vermont: Garden Way Publishers, 1975.

GREEN MANURE

ALTER, RICHARD, and RAYMOND, RICHARD. *Improving Garden Soil with Green Manure: A Guide for the Home Gardener.* Charlotte, Vermont: Garden Way Publishers, 1974.

PLANT PROTECTION

Organic Gardening and Farming Editors, VEPSEN, ROGER, ed. *Organic Plant Protection.* Emmaus, Pennsylvania: Rodale Press, Inc., 1976.

PHILBRICK, HELEN, and GREGG, RICHARD B. *Companion Plants and How to Use Them.* Old Greenwich, Connecticut: Devin-Adair Company, 1966.

WESTCOTT, CYNTHIA. *The Gardener's Bug Book.* New York: Doubleday, 1973.

COOKING AND PRESERVING

The Ball Blue Book. Muncie, Indiana: Ball Brothers Company. (How to can, pickle, freeze and preserve fruits and vegetables. Lots of good recipes. $1.00 from Ball Brothers Company, Muncie, Indiana 47302.)

DAVIS, ADELLE. *Let's Cook It Right.* New York: Harcourt Brace Jovanovich, 1962.

HERTZBERG, RUTH; VAUGHAN, BEATRICE; and GREENE, JANET. *Putting Food By.* Brattleboro, Vermont: Stephen Greene, 1973.

Organic Gardening and Farming Staff, CAROL STONER, ed. *Stocking Up: How to Preserve the Foods You Grow, Naturally.* Emmaus, Pennsylvania: Rodale Press, Inc., 1973.

ENCYCLOPEDIAS

Organic Gardening and Farming Staff, RODALE, J. I., ed. *The Encyclopedia of Organic Gardening.* Emmaus, Pennsylvania: Rodale Press, © 1959.

TIEDJENS, VICTOR A. *The Vegetable Encyclopedia & Gardener's Guide.* New York: Barnes & Noble, 1975. (Much worthwhile information here; I just ignore the occasional recommendations to use pesticides and chemical fertilizers.)

142

143